A CHAUCER SELECTION

LIFE, LITERATURE, AND THOUGHT LIBRARY

General Editor
PROFESSOR VIVIAN DE SOLA PINTO, D.PHIL.
PROFESSOR OF ENGLISH IN THE UNIVERSITY OF NOTTINGHAM

A Chaucer Selection

EDITED BY

L. J. LLOYD

GEORGE G. HARRAP & CO. LTD

LONDON TORONTO WELLINGTON SYDNEY

First published 1952
by GEORGE G. HARRAP & CO. LTD
182 High Holborn, London, W.C.1

Dewey Decimal Cassification: 821.17

*Composed in Garamond type and printed by
Western Printing Services Ltd, Bristol*
Made in Great Britain

FOREWORD

THIS series aims at presenting in an attractive form English texts which have not only intrinsic merit as literature, but which are also valuable as manifestations of the spirit of the age in which they were written. The plan was inspired by the desire to break away from the usual annotated edition of English classics and to provide a series of books illustrating some of the chief developments in English civilization since the Middle Ages. Each volume will have a substantial introduction, which will relate the author to the main currents of contemporary life and thought, and which will be an important part of the book. Notes, where given, will be brief, stimulating, and designed to encourage the spirit of research in the student. It is believed that these books will be of especial value to students in universities and in the upper forms of schools, and that they will also appeal very much to the general reader.

Grateful acknowledgment is made of the valuable help given to the series in its early stages by Mr S. E. Buckley.

VIVIAN DE SOLA PINTO
General Editor

PREFACE

I HAVE been very conscious of the responsibilities—and the hazards—involved in the preparation of this anthology. For if the reader does not, in the end, turn with a pleasant sense of anticipation to Chaucer's collected works, I shall have missed my mark. The selections will not perhaps satisfy every one; least of all those to whom extracts from a single author are in any case anathema. But I hope they will be found to present a fair and balanced picture of their author.

My debts are naturally very numerous, and though I have tried to acknowledge them all, I cannot but suppose that there will be some omissions. For these I ask indulgence. The Clarendon Press, Oxford, has been kind enough to allow me to reproduce the text of *The Works of Geoffrey Chaucer*, edited by W. W. Skeat (1894–97); and I have added, in the notes, a few variants which may be of interest.

I cannot omit a very grateful reference to my colleagues and pupils, with whom I have talked and argued Chaucer for so many years. But my greatest debt is to my friend and master H. S. Bennett, who first introduced me to the world of Chaucer twenty-five years ago, and whose precept and example have been a steady encouragement ever since.

L. J. LLOYD

EXETER, 1952

CONTENTS

INTRODUCTION

CHAUCER AND HIS WORLD

THOMAS HOCCLEVE, once Clerk in the Privy Seal Office of
Richard II and Henry IV, has perhaps few claims to make on
the present-day reader of poetry. But he has earned the grati-
tude of all lovers of Chaucer for the portrait of his "maister
dere and fader reverent" which in a happy hour he caused to be
inserted in the manuscript of his *De Regimine Principum*, now
in the British Museum.[1] It is a charming and skilful piece of
work, convincing us at once of its authenticity, if for no
better reason than that it tallies so exactly with Chaucer's own
description of himself in *The Canterbury Tales*:

> Whan seyd was al this miracle, every man
> As sobre was, that wonder was to see,
> Til that our hoste japen tho bigan,
> And than at erst he loked up-on me,
> And seyde thus, 'what man artow?' quod he;
> 'Thou lokest as thou woldest finde an hare,
> For ever up-on the ground I see thee stare.

> Approche neer, and loke up merily.
> Now war yow, sirs, and lat this man have place;
> He in the waast is shape as wel as I;
> This were a popet in an arm t'enbrace
> For any womman, smal and fair of face,
> He semeth elvish by his contenaunce,
> For un-to no wight dooth he daliaunce.

Prologue to "Sir Thopas," ll. 1–14.[2]

[1] This is not, of course, the only portrait of Chaucer in existence. See
Brusendorff, *The Chaucer Tradition* (Oxford University Press, 1925), pp. 13–27.
"That Chaucer was about five feet six inches in height was estimated when his
bones were accidently uncovered in digging the grave for Robert Browning in
Westminster Abbey." J. M. Manly, *Canterbury Tales* (Henry Holt and Co.,
New York, 1928), p. 37.

[2] Line references given in the Introduction refer to the complete edition of
Chaucer's works and not to the selection presented in this book.

Yet it may be that this vivid little painting, priceless though it is, has done Chaucer some disservice. For unless we are careful, our first instinct is to think of him as an old man; to forget that he was ever young. And although it is proper for us to revere him as the father of English poetry it is also worth remembering that he first steps on to the stage of history dressed as a page in a noble household, wearing a pair of red and black breeches.[1]

The fact is, that if we are to understand Chaucer at all we shall be obliged to make a continual effort of the imagination, and even then admit to ourselves that we are probably a long way from the truth. He died some six hundred years ago, and his world was not our world. His attitude to this world, the sort of thing which went on in his head when he got up in the morning (roused, perhaps, by the impatient voice of his wife)[2] and looked out through his window at fourteenth-century London—most of this is beyond us, because we are not medieval. But if we honestly admit that we shall be obliged to travel—for part of the way at least—*sub nocte per umbram*, we need not on that account suppose that the journey is not worth the making, or that there are no Delectable Mountains ahead of us.

At the outset we shall be obliged to observe that the very foundations of the universe have shifted since Chaucer's day. He believed, as did every one else, that the earth was the fixed centre of the cosmos, round which revolved

. . . the spheres of the seven then known planets, of which the sun and the moon were two. Beyond these seven planetary spheres lay the sphere of the fixed stars. Beyond that in turn, and carrying along with it in its 'diurnal sway' the eight spheres which lay within it, moved the *primum mobile*, a ninth sphere with which, to account for certain planetary eccentricities, the Middle Ages had supplemented the Ptolemaic system. We

---

[1] These breeches and his shoes cost three shillings.
[2] *The Hous of Fame*, II, ll. 560–566. See p. 38.

must think, in a word, of Chaucer's universe as geocentric—the 'litel erthe,' encompassed by 'thilke speres thryes three.'[1]

Further, the sphere of the fixed stars, the Zodiac, was divided into twelve parts, or 'signs': Ram, Bull, Twins, Crab, Lion, Virgin, Scales, Scorpion, Archer, Goat, Water-carrier, and Fishes. Each sign, with its constellation, had its own character and quality. So too had each planet. And as the planets passed through the signs these qualities underwent important changes. Important, because to the men and women of the Middle Ages "this brave o'erhanging firmament, this majestical roof fretted with golden fire" was very much more than a beautiful and awe-inspiring spectacle. For they were all in close personal contact with it. Planet and star shed a direct influence on human life, and had to be taken most carefully into account, since this influence continued from birth to death.

Astrology, therefore, was for most of Chaucer's contemporaries a very real department of knowledge, a true science.

And so it followed that there was throughout life a proper astrological time for everything. To perform an action at the wrong time might be disastrous. The Doctor of Phisyk was quite as interested in horoscopes as in medicines, for if the former were neglected the latter might be useless.[2] Pandarus, setting out on a visit to Criseyde,

> . . . caste and knew in good plyt was the mone
> To doon viage,

—taking a normal and elementary precaution. Exactly how much Chaucer himself subscribed to all this it is difficult to say. What is clear, however, is that he was profoundly interested in almost every department of medieval science and philosophy. His work is full of references, not only to the whole body of astrological science, but to medieval speculation about the

[1] J. L. Lowes, *Geoffrey Chaucer* (Oxford University Press, 1934), p. 8.
[2] "Prologue," ll. 414–417.

significance of dreams, the nature of Heaven and Hell, predes-
tination and free-will, alchemy, and, indeed, almost every
topic which might attract the curious and intelligent inquirer
in the fourteenth century.

And as the universe was somehow more friendly and
comprehensible to medieval men and women that it can ever
be to us, so too religion wore a more homely face. God and
His saints, the Devil and his minions, were close and familiar,
an intimate part of daily life. There is perhaps little reason to
suppose that there was more true piety in the Middle Ages
than there is to-day. But the Church was something with
which every one had to reckon, whether he would or no.
Heaven and Hell were clearly defined realities, and the Church
could ensure a safe passage to the first and offer immunity
from the second, though it is true that some theologians
were inclined to take a gloomy view of anyone's chances of
salvation.[1] The Church held a virtual monopoly of learning
and instruction; the monasteries were often great landowners
and employers of labour. In twelfth-century London there
were 136 churches and 13 monasteries, together with the great
Cathedral of St Paul.

But more than this, the parish church was the real centre
of community life in an England which was predominantly
agricultural, and where even the largest towns still preserved
something of their village origins.

It is easy to over-simplify this picture of a people accepting
without question the literal truths of the Bible and the injunc-
tions of their spiritual advisers, delighting in the lives of the
saints and in stories of miracles and divine intervention,
looking to their parish church as an unshakeable rock in a
sea of doubt and trouble. But in the main it is a true picture.[2]
Where there was criticism—and it is as well to remember

[1] See G. G. Coulton, *The Mediæval Scene* (Cambridge University Press, 1930),
p. 19.
[2] See H. S. Bennett, *Chaucer and the Fifteenth Century* (Oxford University Press,
1947), p. 16.

that all nonconformity was heresy[1]—it normally resolved itself into expressions of dissatisfaction with institutions or persons rather than with a rejection of doctrine. A man might be bitterly resentful of the power of monastery or bishop, or declaim against ignorant or unchaste priests, or even plead for the right to read and interpret the Bible for himself. But there were few who would go further than this, and where Chaucer has occasion to depict those to whom religion was a mockery and truth as naught he leaves us in no doubt as to where he takes his own stand. And he speaks for the orthodox majority of his countrymen.

It is broadly true to say that the structure of society in Chaucer's time was what it had been for three centuries past. Nor is this surprising when we reflect that this society was firmly and almost exclusively based on the holding of land. There is, indeed, a sense in which every fourteenth-century Englishman was a countryman, whether he was a citizen of York or Exeter or the inhabitant of a small village lost in the depths of the country.

England was a land of small communities of peasant-farmers, self-contained and largely self-supporting, which were often isolated from one another by large tracks of virgin forest. Roads were few and bad, apart from the great main highways, but though some villagers no doubt stayed in their own neighbourhood all their lives there was more travel in medieval England than is sometimes supposed, with friars, pilgrims, pedlars, great nobles and their retinues, merchants, students—and rogues and vagabonds—continually on the move.

These village groups, sometimes of not much more than four hundred souls, were ruled by the lord of the manor, from whom the peasants held their land, and whose power over their lives and fortunes—at any rate at the beginning of our period—

[1] At the same time, the structure of medieval thought left room for a wide variety of philosophical speculation.

was absolute. The peasant cultivator was literally bound to the soil, *adscriptus glebæ*. He could not leave his scattered strips of ground on the open field and go to another village, or marry off his daughter, without the lord's consent. He was obliged to grind his corn at the lord's mill, and to give him a certain fixed proportion of labour during the year, to use—for a consideration—his oxen and farm implements, and so on. Yet conditions had eased a good deal in many parts of the country by Chaucer's time, and by no means all farmers were serfs. Many, indeed, were substantial yeomen, on the way to becoming landed gentlemen in their own right, though the story is too long to tell here. And although the peasant's lot was often hard—and sometimes desperate—we need not suppose that the typical English village in the Middle Ages was a scene of permanent gloom and resentment. No doubt there were harsh and unreasonable landlords here and there, but Englishmen have not changed radically in the short space of six hundred years, and it does not require remarkable intelligence to grasp the fact that the best work is done by happy and contented workmen, and that every one has a limit beyond which he will neither go nor be driven. The briefest of comparisons between the Jacquerie in France and the Peasants' Revolt in England will serve to make the point abundantly clear.

There is, in fact, a good deal of evidence that medieval village life was by no means without its compensations. Where the feeling of community is strong, and self-sufficiency a fact, a sense of pride and well-being is likely to follow. Langland's picture of country life is beyond question true, but it is not quite the whole picture. Merry England is not entirely a myth, and as long as there was enough to eat and drink country-folk had little difficulty in finding amusement, though no doubt some of it would bear a little hardly on our sensitive nerves to-day.

Throughout his life Chaucer derived never-ending pleasure

from the sights and sounds of the countryside, and it is a commonplace that he has left us some of the most exquisite descriptions of birds, trees, and flowers in the language. Yet it is true to say that he had no real interest in either country life or country people. He was a townsman, a courtier, and a man of business, better pleased with towered cities and the busy hum of men than with the solitude of the woods and fields. He tells us himself that he often enjoyed a walk in the meadows as a relief from too much reading, but he would have been as miserable in a village as Herrick pretended to be in his "dull Devonshire" of the seventeenth century.

But it is not enough merely to say that Chaucer was a townsman. He was, first and foremost, a Londoner, dominated from his earliest years by the sights and sounds of what by medieval standards was a great city. To us, no doubt, it would seem somewhat parochial and pleasantly countrified, with its mere 40,000[1] souls and encircling walls. It was certainly small enough to be taken in as a whole, even by a small boy, particularly when that boy was Geoffrey Chaucer. He could wander about, eager, sharp-eyed, and inquiring, storing up this and that in his remarkable memory; the busy life of the streets, the unending fascination of the water-front. And the countryside came up almost to his very door.

This was a gay, noisy, prosperous, and powerful community. There were shops everywhere—fish-shops in Fish Street, corn-shops on Cornhill, leather-shops in Saddlers' Row. Tradesmen stood by the open stalls, shouting their wares to attract the passer-by:

> Cooks and their men cried, 'Hot pies, hot!
> Good pork and geese: come dine, come!'
> Taverners told them the same tale;
> 'White wine from Alsace and red wine from Gascony,
> From the Rhine and La Rochelle, to digest the roast meat.'[2]

[1] It is always difficult to be precise about medieval figures, but this is probably a fair estimate. Even so, London was over three times as large as any other English city.

[2] Langland, *Piers Plowman*, Prologue, 224–228.

Games were played in the streets; in winter there was skating on the frozen marshes. There were maypoles and dancing, festivals and processions. A rough and unruly scene, no doubt, by modern standards, and one often enough darkened by crime or accident, fire or pestilence. But life was vigorous and robust, for only the fittest could survive in conditions such as these.[1]

The essential feature of trade in town and city was the organization of all business into gilds. The members of these gilds were skilled craftsmen—the unskilled worker had no say in the conduct of affairs—whose object it was not only to protect their own interests but to ensure a high standard in the quality of the goods they sold and to deal fairly with the public. Such, at any rate, was their assured intention, but, as Manly reminds us,

> It is a mistake to believe, as some enthusiastic writers on the Middle Ages apparently do, that the mediæval craftsman was an artist interested primarily in maintaining high quality in all his materials and honesty and beauty in all his workmanship. The records of mediæval gilds and the ordinances of the towns are largely devoted to efforts to prevent cheating and frauds of all sorts in materials and workmanship.[2]

Chaucer himself shows us more than once that he knew something of the tricks of the wine-trade.[3] But there is no need to press the point too far in either direction. We may agree that the medieval craftsman was normally an artist, and often a very great one, and yet face the undoubted fact that the jerry-builder was not unknown even in the Age of Faith.

Chaucer's father was a typical example of the substantial London tradesman, and of that powerful middle class which

---

[1] See L. F. Salzman, *English Life in the Middle Ages* (Oxford University Press, 1926), pp. 80–87.

[2] *Op. cit.*, pp. 53–54.

[3] We remember, for example, his detailed knowledge of the various sorts of wine popular in his day: "The Pardoner's Tale," ll. 234–244. He had often seen these wines unshipped at the quayside.

had by the fourteenth century begun to invade the realm
hitherto occupied almost exclusively by those whose distinction of birth and landed possessions (it was indeed almost
impossible to think of the one without the other) had for
centuries placed them in a class apart. Ever since the days
when merchants and traders had been attracted to little towns
springing up near good harbours, navigable rivers, fords and
bridges, or great monasteries—had stayed to see them develop
as markets for the sale of the produce of neighbouring villages
and farms, and had fought with king or lord or abbot for the
right to act as a body[1]—the middle classes had been steadily
growing in wealth and importance.

John Chaucer was no Dick Whittington, nor was he of the
standing of Sir John Philipot of the Grocers' Company, who
joined with two other great merchants, Brembre and Wal-
worth, in lending over a quarter of a million pounds (in
modern money) to the young Richard II. But he was a man
of considerable substance, deputy to the King's Butler between
1347 and 1349, able to turn his son into a gentleman, and to
number among his descendants members of the Royal house
itself.[2]

Chaucer has given us in the Prologue an unforgettable
portrait of one of these sagacious and worthy men, with his
forked beard, Flemish beaver hat, and stately bearing, and it
is perhaps surprising that we do not hear more of those noble
burgesses the Weaver, Dyer, and Tapestry-maker, each of
whom "was shaply for to been an alderman."[3] But in fact he
says comparatively little about the trade and merchants of
London, in spite of his deep and first-hand knowledge of them.
For all that, London gave him much. Above all, it brought
him into close and daily contact with the men and women
whose habits and qualities he was to be the first Englishman
to chronicle in all their infinite variety.

[1] See G. G. Coulton, *op. cit.*, pp. 51–56.
[2] See Manly, *Canterbury Tales*, pp. 36–37.
[3] Prologue to *The Canterbury Tales*, l. 372.

EARLY WRITINGS

Exactly when he began to interest himself in writing we do
not know; indeed, we know practically nothing of his first
twenty years. Even the date of his birth is uncertain, though
we shall probably not be far out if we put it somewhere about
the year 1343. Nor do we know where he went to school,
though Manly has pointed out that there were three schools
within easy walking distance of Thames Street, where (very
probably) Chaucer was born: St Mary le Bow, St Paul's
Cathedral School, and the school of the Chapel Royal.[1]

But we may be certain of one thing—that he worked hard
during these early years. He was never a finished scholar, at
any rate in the academic sense of the phrase, but his appearance
later as a singularly well-read man, familiar with Latin, French,
and Italian, argues an acquaintance with book-learning which
could hardly have been acquired without a good deal of hard
and wide reading. And perhaps his unknown teachers deserve
a little posthumous credit for this, and for instilling into their
pupil that passion for literature which remained with him to
the end of his life.[2]

Chaucer's father, as we have seen, had close connexions
with the Court, and it was no doubt for this reason that when
Geoffrey was old enough to go out into the world (to medieval
parents that time arrived for their children very early indeed)
he was able to procure for him a place in the household of
Elizabeth, Countess of Ulster. This was a fine start for any
boy, and one which, as the son of a tradesman, he might
otherwise have found it difficult to come by—though it is true

---

[1] *Op. cit.*, p. 7.

[2] For Chaucer's reading see Lowes, *Geoffrey Chaucer*, pp. 56–91. There is also
a tradition that he studied law at the Inner Temple. Thomas Speght, whose
edition of Chaucer appeared in 1598, speaks of one "Master Buckley," who
"did see a recorde in the same howse, where Geffrye Chaucer was fined two
shillinges for beatinge a Franciscane Fryer in fletestreate." See Manly, *op. cit.*,
p. 25.

that Edward III was on excellent terms with the London merchants, and there were signs that the rigid barriers of caste were yielding to financial pressure. He thus gained an early introduction, under the happiest of auspices, into that world of great affairs in which he was later to be so much at home. In 1357, for instance, he spent Christmas at Hatfield, the Countess's Yorkshire house (where one of the guests was John of Gaunt, then Earl of Richmond), and the records show that he received an allowance of two shillings and sixpence "for necessaries" during his stay there. No doubt he accompanied his royal mistress on some of her other travels, to Reading, perhaps, and to Stratford-atte-Bowe, and back to London again. And we may be reasonably sure that he played an eager, if humble, part in more than one of the magnificent entertainments in which that great lady delighted.

For it was in ways such as these, and in great houses like Hatfield, that the sons of the nobility (and those privileged to be of their company) acquired—sometimes not without pain— an understanding of the true meaning of Courtoisie. They performed the tasks required of them, and watched carefully all that went on, learning to serve that they might one day command. It would be difficult to imagine a more exciting life for a young man on the threshold of a promising career, and we know that Chaucer made the best possible use of his opportunities. For the result was that we see him now as the most urbane, the most truly 'gentle,' of all our poets.

His sixty years were full of employment. He was page, courtier, soldier (and prisoner-of-war), secret-service agent, controller of Customs, Clerk of Works, Member of Parliament. The list of his many appointments is too long to quote here.[1] But that he was an extremely busy public servant for most of his life admits of no question. His literary activity was a hobby and relaxation; and he wrote during whatever leisure he could contrive from the pressure of his official duties. This is not to

[1] See the list of the main events in his career at p. 63.

suggest that his fame as a poet did not occasionally bring him into greater notice than might otherwise have been his, or that it might not have been the indirect means of filling that purse which was sometimes so light. There was, after all, more than one way of approaching a patron in the Middle Ages. But, on the whole, the day of the professional author as we understand him was as yet a long way off, and the peculiar graciousness of Chaucer's art is at any rate partly due to the fact that it is the work of a man who wrote to please himself and his friends, in his own time, and in his own fashion.

There were, broadly speaking, two courses open to a young and cultivated Englishman of the mid-fourteenth century who wished to write poetry. He might follow the traditional road, and use the alliterative measure long hallowed by history and association.[1] Or he might imitate as well as he could in English the fashionable poetry of Machaut,[2] Deschamps, Froissart, and their contemporaries in France.

This poetry was not, perhaps, of the highest quality, though Deschamps occasionally came near to greatness. It lacked strength, and rarely attempted to penetrate deeply below the upper surfaces of emotion and feeling. Elegance and charm, however, it possessed in abundance, and it was often extremely amusing. Most important of all, its exponents were masters of their craft. New lyric forms had appeared during the early part of the fourteenth century: the rondel, the ballade, the chant-royal, the virelai, and so on. Most of them were to enjoy a continued popularity for the next hundred years. Chaucer was attracted towards the richness and variety of this new poetry, both by training and inclination, as well as environment, employment, and instinct. It is well that this was

[1] This is not to lose sight of the fact that rhymed verse had been in constant use for over two centuries.

[2] It was Guillaume de Machaut (c. 1290–1377) whose influence on Chaucer was most marked. He was a fine craftsman, highly versed in the new technique, and he provided Chaucer with precisely the kind of inspiration he most needed. See, for the influence of Machaut and Froissart, G. L. Kittredge, *Chaucer and his Poetry* (Cambridge, Mass., 1939), pp. 54–66.

so, for English verse was sorely in need of rejuvenation. So he applied himself to French poetry; he translated and adapted; he experimented and discarded. And across the Channel his work came in time to be regarded with favour. Secure in his impregnable cultural fortress, Eustace Deschamps could well afford to greet his English disciple with a friendly gesture. We need not see a touch of condescension in his famous "grant translateur, noble Geffroy Chaucier," since Chaucer himself would have been totally unaware of anything of the kind. To him it would have seemed no more than the simple truth, and high praise at that.[1]

THE ROMAUNT OF THE ROSE

Chaucer's most important single production during these first tentative years was his translation of the *Roman de la Rose*, a poem begun during the early part of the thirteenth century by Guillaume de Lorris, a cultivated and sensitive artist, whose vision of the world was gracious and refined to a degree unusual even among the most aristocratic of authors. He describes, in quiet and leisurely fashion, how the Lover, seeking the Rose in the enchanted garden, is constantly baffled and turned aside before he can attain his end, though he is permitted a taste of future joys.

Émile Faguet thus describes the theme:

The centre figure of the whole is a being so abstract that he has no individual name; he is only called the Lover, and typifies Love itself. Then, most difficult to win, and surrounded by a thousand obstacles which must be overcome, a new kind of Holy Grail, there is the Rose, which typifies Beauty.

Leagued against the Lover, that is, against love, are certain monsters, such as Hatred, Treason, Avarice, Envy, Hypocrisy, Poverty, Shame, Fear, Jealousy, Dangier (also known as power, authority, paternal or otherwise), etc. The friends and helpers

[1] The whole poem can be conveniently studied in the *Oxford Book of French Verse*, pp. 11–12. Manly, *op. cit.*, pp. 23–25, prints both the poem and a translation.

of the Lover are benevolent beings such as Youth, Beauty, Nobility of Heart, Generosity, Courtesy, Delight, Enjoyment, who is the bride of Delight, as is natural. These, then, are two opposing camps.

Now the Lady Idleness, the mother of all vices and sins, has led the Lover into the Garden of the Rose. At the outset he is turned from his path after approaching her, but he returns under the protection of Venus and dares to touch the Rose with his lips. And straightway Dangier, Jealousy, Shame, and Slander shut up the Rose in a lofty fortress, and then . . . Guillaume de Lorris died; at least, so his successor who continued the legend relates:

> Cy endroit trépassa Guillaume
> De Lorris, et n'en fit plus psaume,
> Mais après plus de quarante ans
> Maistre Jean de Meung ce romans
> Parfit ainsi comme je treuve;
> Et ici commence son œuvre.[1]

The poem is the mirror of perfection of medieval courtesy. There is no contact with the outside workaday world, but this dreamer keeps a firm hold on the true significance of what he is writing, and makes it abundantly clear that to write in symbol and the similitude of a dream is by no means necessarily the same thing as living with one's head in the clouds.[2]

The work of de Lorris is, however, only one side of the medal. As we have seen, he died before he could finish his story. Forty years later, a poet of a very different sort, Jean de Meung, took up the unfinished fabric, and wove it into a tapestry which would probably have caused its originator no little concern. Jean de Meung was a brilliant and sardonic person, "satirically disposed," as George Saintsbury put it, to a vision of the world very different from that of the quiet and chivalrous de Lorris. His "huge, dishevelled, violent poem of eighteen thousand lines"[3] changes the scene completely. Its

---

[1] *A Literary History of France* (Unwin, 1907), pp. 64–65.

[2] C. S. Lewis's *Allegory of Love* (Oxford University Press, 1936) is indispensable for any study of the *Roman de la Rose*.

[3] C. S. Lewis, *op. cit.*, p. 137.

author discourses in long and leisurely fashion on a variety of contemporary topics. He is at considerable pains to show us that he has at his command all the current notions of philosophy and the natural sciences. But, most important and significant of all, he makes it clear that he takes a low view of womankind; or, at best, a view swayed by the head and not the heart. And it is here above all that there could be no compromise between his work and that of the earlier poet. Jean de Meung was, to put the matter simply, too coarse-fibred to rest content with a scheme at once so subtle and so gracious. Yet although, as Mr Lewis remarks, "it was the misfortune of Jean de Meung to have read and remembered everything,"[1] and to have put most of it into his poem, the story does somehow contrive to move—or at any rate to crawl—forward. The Lover gathers the long-sought-for Rose, and the great quest is at an end, after precisely 22,047 lines.

It is worth while calling to mind the length of this great poem, and reflecting for a moment on the glee with which a medieval reader—or a medieval audience—would settle down comfortably to enjoy a work of such prodigious size. For length itself was a virtue in an age when leisure was plentiful and outside amusements few. Nothing was relished more keenly than instruction conveyed in an agreeable and palatable form. Hence Jean de Meung's many digressions—the Dreamer's conversation with Reason, Bialacoil's discourse on Love, the sermon of Genius, and so on. And hence, incidentally, some of Chaucer's frequent long asides and deviations from the straight path of story-telling, which have caused even his most devout admirers to falter once in a while.

Jean de Meung, then, gave his audience exactly what it desired. He was a resourceful and (according to his lights) a skilful craftsman, eager, inquiring, and enthusiastic, aspiring to omniscience in typical medieval fashion. With little or nothing of the grace of de Lorris, he had much more power. He sums

[1] *Op. cit.*, p. 151.

up the more practical and everyday side of medieval life—the coarser side, if you will—and he provides the perfect foil to the reticent and delicate charm of his predecessor.

Few poems have reflected an age with greater faithfulness than the *Roman de la Rose*, and long and continued popularity was its just reward. Here was something for every one: a never-failing supply of comment, allusion, and anecdote; an epitome of courtly behaviour; an approach to poetry. The added flavour of mystery, of hidden treasure waiting to be discovered by those willing enough to take the necessary pains, was all that was needed for complete success. It is perhaps not too much to say that in the end a close acquaintance with the *Roman de la Rose* was an apprenticeship through which all medieval poets had to pass. Chaucer served his time with the rest, and attended to his business more assiduously than most of them: 1705 lines of the *Roman* in English are there to prove it. But the influence of the poem went much deeper than that. The spirit of the *Roman de la Rose*—the influence now of de Lorris, now of Jean de Meung—became an essential part of the very fibre of his poetry.

We need not linger over his own version, except to admire for a moment the smoothness and clarity of the verse and to marvel at so much technical accomplishment in so young a poet. For it is curiously impersonal: there is little or nothing there which we have now learned to call Chaucerian. But it is very medieval, and not least in its anonymity and complete lack of that 'sense of personality' which we hear so much about nowadays, and of which Dante made such short work in the *De Vulgari Eloquentia*:

But it is in the exercise of the needful caution and discernment that the real difficulty lies; for this can never be attained to without strenuous efforts of genius, constant practice in the art, and the habit of the sciences. And it is those (so equipped) whom the poet in the sixth book of the *Æneid* describes as beloved of God, raised by glowing virtue to the sky, and sons of the Gods, though he is speaking figuratively. And therefore let those who, innocent of art and science, and trusting to genius alone, rush forward to sing of the highest subjects in the highest style, confess their folly and cease from such presumption; and if in their natural sluggishness they are but geese, let them abstain from imitating the eagle soaring to the stars.[1]

Chaucer was equally well aware of the value of sound craftsmanship, and here he was about craftsman's business. To have obtruded his own opinions and observations into the sacred matter of the *Roman* would have seemed to him an act of sheer vandalism. He approached such a distinguished work of art with all the reverence proper to it. And he laboured hard to convey it to English readers as clearly and as succinctly as he could—a task not easy.

It was most competently and charmingly done. Yet, as far as we know, he worked at the *Roman* just as long as he felt he was getting from it something vitally necessary to him, and no longer. This, as we shall see, was his way. He was continually pressing forward towards new experiences, new problems. We do not normally associate Chaucer with restlessness, yet his poetic path is strewn with discarded experiments. No other poet of his standing has been responsible for so many unfinished works.

His careful translation is, none the less, a great achievement, and we may reasonably suppose that as he worked away at this delightful and formidable task he turned aside now and again to attempt something on a smaller scale, and more immediately rewarding. It is true that we have lost almost all his early translations and imitations. Nothing in this kind now exists which we can be absolutely certain Chaucer wrote before he was thirty. Many poems no doubt perished in the hands of those for whom they were made. But some have survived, and we may, if we choose, decide that a few of them are maturer

[1] *The Latin Works of Dante*, translated by A. G. Ferrers Howell (Temple Classics, 1904), pp. 79–80.

versions of other songs now lost. The little epilogue or tail-piece to *The Parlement of Foules* may be one.

These were trifles, no doubt; idle things to amuse an idle hour. Still, by constant and assiduous practice, in this vein and in many others, Chaucer was slowly acquiring that technique which was essential to his purpose. Everything was welcome, and might be useful: a ballade, a sermon, a virelai; a whole *Roman de la Rose*.

THE BOKE OF THE DUCHESSE

One thing at any rate is beyond question. Chaucer emerged from his long stay in the enchanted garden the devoted servant of Allegory. Many years were to pass before this fascinating and seductive literary form ceased to claim the attention of his mind and heart. *The Boke of the Duchesse, The Parlement of Foules, The Hous of Fame,* and *The Legende of Good Women* are all fruits of his discipleship.

We need not, however, suppose that Chaucer was either an unwilling or a passive servant. For it is clear that in these years he slipped into allegorical writing as easily as a man slips into an old coat. It was easy and comfortable wear, clothing and protecting his thoughts, but not restricting them. Safe within these dignified and reputable bounds, he could range about freely, yet always with that comforting sense of being on the right path which a sense of tradition gives to a young writer.

The Boke of the Duchesse, which appeared somewhere about 1369, is a fascinating example of a great poet's first steps on his own account. "It lacks great distinction." "It is largely deriva-tive." So we are told. But it is extremely difficult to think of anyone else who could have written it. It is full of that indefinable blend of innocence, grace, shrewdness, spontaneous gaiety and seriousness which is no doubt part of the essence of medievalism at its best—but which is also something that nowadays we find ourselves describing simply as Chaucerian.

Moreover, it shows us clearly that he has now absorbed, and made his own, the great tradition of Courtly Love (and courtly writing) which, deriving ultimately from Ovid's *Ars Amatoria,* was developed by the Troubadour poets of Languedoc, elaborated and refined by Chrétien de Troyes and others in the twelfth century, and then given its final form by the authors of the *Roman de la Rose.*

It is a strange, unreal, and fascinating world in which we find ourselves if we look for a moment at the work of Arnaut Daniel, Bernart de Ventadour, Peire Vidal, and their companions. Perhaps for a moment we may be tempted to smile at the intense seriousness with which these priests of Love go about their appointed tasks, but there is a curious beauty in the poems which flower from this most aristocratic and seemingly artificial of literary conventions.

It appeared quite suddenly, at the end of the eleventh century, with William of Poitiers, and it changed at least one aspect of European literature for ever. For the lyrics of the Troubadours are by no means what they may first appear to be: the idle—if pleasant—amusement of a group of polite and courtly persons who studiously avert their gaze from life as it really is, have much more time on their hands than they know what to do with, and are devoting themselves to a form of activity so artificial in character that it must surely be doomed to speedy and complete oblivion.

On the contrary. This hot-house plant was in reality surprisingly tough in fibre. The essential quality of Troubadour poetry was something which European literature had never experienced before, and has never allowed to disappear from that time to our own day.

French poets, in the eleventh century, discovered or invented, or were the first to express, that romantic species of passion which English poets were still writing about in the nineteenth. They effected a change which has left no corner of our ethics, our imagination, or our daily life untouched, and they erected barriers between us and the classical past or the Oriental present. Compared with this revolution the Renaissance is a mere ripple on the surface of literature.[1]

The Troubadours were rigidly bound by laws of their own making, and although these rules may look somewhat strange —and maybe even foolish—to the twentieth-century reader who has Shakespeare and Fielding and Dickens and Thackeray on his shelves, we cannot afford to pass them by if we wish to understand *The Boke of the Duchesse*, *The Parlement of Foules*, and *Troilus and Criseyde*. For Chaucer was—all his life, and first and foremost—the poet of Love, and though his conception of love broadened and deepened as he grew older the essential features of the courtly tradition are always to be discerned beneath the surface.

It will therefore be worth while examining for a moment some aspects of the Troubadour's world.

In the first place, the lover admitted the absolute sovereignty of his lady, who was beauty's self, and whose lightest word was immutable law. To her he offered undying fidelity, and he asked for no reward save what she in her infinite kindness might think fit to bestow on him. He offered her abject obedience, and he feared her slightest rebuke more than death. More than this, he promised complete and utter secrecy in all things, for the betrayal of a confidence or a favour was immeasurably the most heinous crime in the lover's calendar. But a confidant there must be, to serve as a link between the Troubadour and his divinity, to hear 'complaints,' soothe despair, and carry letters on the lines of the 'epistles'—the *Heroides*—of Ovid. Yet all this, it must be noted, had nothing whatever to do with marriage. Whatever the right true end of love might be, it was not that. Indeed, the lover normally paid court to a woman who was already married—though it is the rival, and not the husband, whom he fears. Still, to quote Mr C. S. Lewis once again:

[1] C. S. Lewis, *op. cit.*, p. 4.

. . . if he is ethically careless, he is no light-hearted gallant: his love is represented as a despairing and tragical emotion—or almost despairing, for he is saved from complete despair by his faith in the God of Love who never betrays his faithful worshippers and who can subjugate the cruellest beauties.[1]

That then, in brief, was love, as the eleventh- and twelfth-century poets saw it, and as Chaucer was to see it (in a modified and altered shape) three centuries later.

But this was not the whole of the matter. It was not sufficient merely to be a lover. To be in love was to be a poet, a master of the highly complicated art of rhetoric and the whole business of courtly writing. For love demanded the highest skill of which a man was capable, a long and hard apprenticeship to the craft, constant humility and sacrifice.

So it comes about that towards the end of his life Chaucer can proudly boast that he has

> . . . told of loveres up and doun
> Mo than Ovyde made of mencioun
> In his Epistelles, that been ful olde.

A man might well be content with such an epitaph; it would be an ample reward for a lifetime of assiduous and devoted labour.[2]

One thing more may be said. Artificial and unreal though it might seem—immoral even, as some might think it—the tradition of courtly love was one thing above all else. It was civilized. It preached affection, humility, unselfishness, and true courtesy in an age when such things were often conspicuously absent, when marriage was almost exclusively a matter of exchange and barter, and when Love was indeed locked out

---

[1] *Op. cit.*, p. 3.
[2] For an excellent summary of the meaning of medieval rhetoric, see *Troilus and Criseyde*, ed. R. C. Goffin (Oxford University Press, 1935), pp. xi–xiv. It is interesting to reflect that many of Chaucer's happiest—and apparently most spontaneous—utterances were firmly based on the elaborate rules which he had learned from such masters as Martianus Capella and Geoffrey de Vinsauf. These feats of technical skill gave, of course, a double pleasure to his contemporaries, who were listening to brilliant variations on familiar themes.

of the council chamber. And it enjoined upon men a respect for women which, though it might have begun as a charming literary convention—mere lip-service—became in the end one of the corner-stones of European civilization.[1]

The Boke of the Duchesse begins, as all medieval allegories should begin, in May—"that mother is of monthes glade."

Spring, a poet, and a dream—so the stage is set. Chaucer cannot sleep, he tells us, so he takes up a book, and the book is the sad story of Ceyx and Alcyone, their great love for one another, and Alcyone's wonderful dream. One dream leads to another. Chaucer himself falls asleep, and the story begins.

> Me thoughte thus:—that hit was May,
> And in the dawning ther I lay,
> Me mette thus, in my bed al naked:—
> I loked forth, for I was waked
> With smale foules a gret hepe,
> That had affrayed me out of slepe
> Through noyse and swetnesse of hir song;
> *ll.* 291–297

As he lies there he hears the sound of a horn, and, as he says somewhat oddly,

> I was right glad, and up anoon;
> I took my hors, and forth I wente
> Out of my chambre; I never stente
> Til I com to the feld withoute.
> *ll.* 356–359

There he is told that the Emperor Octavian is out for a day's sport. But the hart gets away, and the hunt is recalled. Chaucer wanders away through the woods, and suddenly comes upon

> . . . a man in blak,
> That sat and had y-turned his bak
> To an oke, an huge tree.
> *ll.* 445–447

[1] See Nevill Coghill, *The Poet Chaucer* (Oxford University Press, 1949), pp. 15–21, for some admirable observations on the theory of courtly love.

This knight, for such he is, is bitterly lamenting the loss of his lady

> That was so fayr, so fresh, so free,
> So good, that men may wel y-see
> Of al goodnesse she had no mete!—
> *ll.* 484–486

Chaucer approaches, so obviously full of sympathy that the knight unburdens himself of his sorrow, and tells him the whole story: the timid approach to one whose beauty and charm were without peer, the first uncompromising "nay!," the long period of humble service and unswerving devotion, the final mercy of friendship. All this is certainly both allegorical and traditional, but the poem has a substratum of hard fact, for the Black Knight is John of Gaunt, and the lady is the Duchess Blanche, who died in 1369. Nor is the poet himself entirely anonymous. Once at least he steps out of the tapestry and speaks in his own voice and person:

> But men mighte axe me, why so
> I may not slepe, and what me is?
> But natheles, who aske this
> Leseth his asking trewely.
> My-selven can not telle why
> The sooth; but trewely, as I gesse,
> I holdë hit be a siknesse
> That I have suffred this eight yere,
> And yet my bote is never the nere;
> For ther is phisicien but oon,
> That may me hele; but that is doon.
> Passe we over until eft;
> That wil not be, moot nede be left;
> Our first matere is good to kepe.
> *ll.* 30–43

Surely this "eight yere" is not convention? There is a touch of unusual precision here, and, since Chaucer is not now translating, may we not perhaps assume that this is a reference, fleeting and reticent though it is, to a love-passage of his own youth? And as for precision, what of the little hound which comes up to the poet as he walks away from his tree?

> I was go walked fro my tree,
> And as I wente, ther cam by me
> A whelp, that fauned me as I stood,
> That hadde y-folowed, and coude no good.
> Hit com and creep to me as lowe,
> Right as hit hadde me y-knowe,
> Hild doun his heed and joyned his eres,
> And leyde al smothe doun his heres.
> I wolde han caught hit, and anoon
> Hit fledde, and was fro me goon.
>
> *ll.* 387–396

The importance of this vignette is out of all proportion to its size. It offers us for the first time—quite apart from the ease and naturalness of its language—an illustration of Chaucer's "seeing eye," a foretaste of that remarkable command of essential detail and power of vivid description which were later to serve him so well.

Nor is this all. *The Boke of the Duchesse* is clear proof that by 1370 Chaucer was well on the road towards that mastery of conversational verse which is seemingly so easy to achieve, but which at its best—Chaucer's best, a triumph of technical skill—was to be one of the glories of *Troilus* and *The Canterbury Tales*.

> 'Why so?' quod he; 'it is nat so;
> Thou wost ful litel what thou menest;
> I have lost more than thou wenest.'
> 'Lo, sir, how may that be?' quod I;
> 'Good sir, tel me al hoolly
> In what wyse, how, why, and wherfore
> That ye have thus your blisse lore.'
> 'Blythly,' quod he, 'com sit adoun;
> I telle thee up condicioun
> That thou hoolly, with al thy wit,
> Do thyn entent to herkene hit.'
> 'Yis, sir.' 'Swere thy trouthe ther-to.'

'Gladly.' 'Do than holde her-to!'
'I shal right blythly, so god me save,
Hoolly, with al the witte I have,
Here yow, as wel as I can.'

ll. 742–757

He handles his hard-won weapons with deceptive ease, and it is
pleasant to see him for the first time as a poet in his own right,
dutifully performing what was required of him as a newcomer,
but agreeably conscious of his own individuality as a veritable
'auctor' and allegorist.

Allusions abound, therefore. Authorities crop up at every
turn. The medieval delight in catalogues is illustrated with an
enthusiasm which is almost comic in the Black Knight's careful
survey of his lady's graces and virtues:

But swich a fairnesse of a nekke
Had that swete, that boon nor brekke
Nas ther non sene, that mis-sat.
Hit was whyt, smothe, streght, and flat,
Withouten hole; and canel-boon,
As by seming, had she noon.
Hir throte, as I have now memoire,
Semed a round tour of yvoire,
Of good gretnesse, and noght to grete.

ll. 939–947

And so on—the whole armoury of a medieval poet is laid out
for our inspection and edification.[1] Autolycus himself could
not have displayed the contents of his knapsack with greater
cheerfulness and delight.

'I leve yow wel, that trewely
Yow thoghte, that she was the beste,
And to beholde the alderfaireste,
Who so had loked with your eyen.'

'With myn? nay, alle that hir seyen
Seyde, and sworen hit was so.
And thogh they ne hadde, I wolde tho
Have loved best my lady fre,

[1] See also ll. 721–741.

C

Thogh I had had al the beautee
That ever had Alcipyades,
And al the strengthe of Ercules,
And therto had the worthinesse
Of Alisaundre, and al the richesse
That ever was in Babiloyne,
In Cartage, or in Macedoyne . . .'
ll. 1048–1062

To a modern reader there is something a little overwhelming about all this, but Chaucer is extremely sensitive to the dignity of the occasion. *The Boke of the Duchesse* was, after all, his first important complimentary poem, destined to reach the ear of no less a person than John of Gaunt himself. He put everything he knew into the making of it; his whole future reputation as a poet might well depend on its success or failure. We do not know what John of Gaunt thought of it, but we are surely entitled to assume that he was not displeased.

THE PARLEMENT OF FOULES

So, in Chaucer's thirtieth year, the long process begins. Allegory succeeds allegory, and at every stage the poet's grip on his material grows stronger; year by year his independence is more marked, his emancipation becomes more and more complete. But the framework, the outward trappings, remains the same.

The beautiful pattern is repeated: Maytime, the singing birds, books, a favourite book, sleep, and a dream. Whatever one may think of conventions in general, here surely is one of the most gracious and rewarding of them all. For all that, dreams are one thing, and dreaminess is another. And Chaucer is wide enough awake when once he is safely through the gates of ivory. He walks briskly about the magic ground, alert, observant, and inquiring; ready to talk, and ready to listen. Ready to laugh, too, and readiest of all, perhaps, to laugh at himself.[1]

Fortune, so they say, favours poets, and Chaucer was certainly as fortunate as any. He always dreams at the right time—invariably arrives just as something interesting is about to happen. As, for example, in *The Parlement of Foules*. He has wandered through the familiar and exquisite countryside, paused long enough to give us a little catalogue of the trees which flourish in that fair region; nodded, as it were, to such old friends as Plesaunce, Curtesye, and Fool-hardinesse; and bowed gravely to Beautee. Then, suddenly, the air is full of the sound of wings. It is St Valentine's day, "Whan every foul cometh ther to chese his make," and there is Dame Nature in the midst, ready to help her impatient subjects, and to approve their choice.

Her main task on this memorable day, is, we find, to arbitrate between three eagles; a royal 'tercel,' or male, a tercel "of lower kinde," and a third, who is accorded no epithet. They are all asking for the favour (one had almost said the hand) of

> A formel egle, of shap the gentileste
> That ever she among hir werkes fonde,
> The most benigne and the goodlieste;
> In hir was every vertu at his reste,
> So ferforth, that Nature hir-self had blisse
> To loke on hir, and ofte hir bek to kisse.
>
> *ll.* 373–378

Each bird asserts his claim with impassioned fervour, yet with great dignity, speaking the language of the Courts of Love;

> Beseching hir of mercy and of grace,
> As she that is my lady sovereyne;
> Or let me dye present in this place.
> For certes, long may I not live in peyne;
> For in myn herte is corven every veyne;
> Having reward al only to my trouthe,
> My dere herte, have on my wo som routhe.
>
> *ll.* 421–427

[1] "Almost all Chaucer's references to himself are ironical."—Kittredge, *Chaucer and his Poetry*, p. 31.

So speaks the royal tercel, opening his heart to such an extent that the lady (unused to such public demonstrations of feeling) is reduced to confusion. But she has a mind of her own, and when all her suitors have had their say she gathers up her courage and takes a firm stand, declaring politely but firmly that she is 'owre young to marry yet.' No high-born maiden could have argued her case better, and, indeed, that is precisely what she is. The scene has changed; the world of the *Roman de la Rose* has vanished away, and we are in fourteenth-century London, where all the courtiers and citizens are wearing fancy-dress. To the casual eye they no doubt appear to be eagles, swans, sparrows, and ducks, but they speak the language of courtesy and the dialect of the London streets. Listen for a moment to the lower elements, anxious to be away with their partners, and caring nothing for chivalry. Here is the plain man's view of courtly love, and all the other nonsense beloved of gentlefolk:

> 'Wel bourded!' quod the doke, 'by my hat!
> That men shulde alwey loven, causeles,
> Who can a reson finde or wit in that?
> Daunceth he mury that is mirtheles?
> Who shulde recche of that is reccheles?
> Ye, quek!' yit quod the doke, ful wel and faire,
> 'There been mo sterres, god wot, than a paire!'
>
> *ll.* 589–595

Chaucer is very much on his own ground here; Chauntecleer and Pertelote are not very far away. Indeed, we are at liberty to think, if we are so minded, that they decided to set up house on this very St Valentine's Day of all days.

The Parlement of Foules is the most successful of all Chaucer's minor poems. It is not too long, and his cherished authorities are kept in their proper places, and serve only to embellish and enrich the narrative. Best of all, Chaucer is here truly himself for the first time, and almost all he was to do later is foreshadowed in one way or another. Shrewd characterization, narrative power, and incisive description, humour, and courtly grace, go hand in hand. There had been nothing even remotely like this in English before.

THE HOUS OF FAME

The idea of a talking bird seems to have exercised a peculiar fascination over Chaucer's mind at this period of his life. For he selects a senior member of the Parlement of Foules—if one may put it so—to be the chief protagonist in another poem written about this time.

The Hous of Fame is a somewhat curious work. As an artistic whole it cannot compare with *The Parlement of Foules*. Even allowing for the fact that it is unfinished, it is shapeless and top-heavy. It contains long stretches of dullness, and there are times when the authorities—Virgil in particular—seem to take the poem out of Chaucer's hands altogether. The allegorical framework creaks now and again, and once, at any rate, it is near to complete collapse.

Chaucer begins with the now familiar questionings as to the nature and true significance of dreams, and it is worth noting that he had much more than the conventional interest in this seductive topic. His own dream, he says, occurred on the tenth day of December, when he was as weary as a pilgrim to the shrine of St Leonard.

He finds himself at once in a temple of glass, dedicated to Venus, who is depicted, as if by an earlier Botticelli,

> Naked fletinge in a see.
> And also on hir heed, pardee,
> Hir rose-garlond whyt and reed,
> And hir comb to kembe hir heed,
> Hir dowves, and daun Cupido,
> Hir blinde sone, and Vulcano,
> That in his face was ful broun.[1]
>
> *Book* I, *ll.* 133–139

[1] Compare "The Knight's Tale," ll. 1097–1098, where the statue of Venus
"... glorious for to see,
Was naked fleting in the large see."

Engraved on a tablet of brass he sees these memorable lines:

> 'I wol now singe, if that I can,
> The armes, and al-so the man,
> That first cam, through his destinee,
> Fugitif of Troye contree,
> In Itaile, with ful moche pyne,
> Unto the strondes of Lavyne.'
>
> *Book* I, *ll.* 143–148

and it is with a sense almost of shock that we hear this famous exordium in the accents of the fourteenth century, and from our own Chaucer into the bargain.

The whole story of the Æneid is now set out before him, and before us in our turn. The tale is told well enough, but we are none the less relieved when Chaucer decides to go out, "right at the wiket," and see if there is anyone about who can tell him exactly where he is. For a time he sees nothing but a drear and sandy waste. Then, to his great dismay, an eagle swoops down from highest heaven, picks him up in its great claws as he runs away in terror, and is off with him in a flash.

It is a dramatic moment, both for Chaucer and for the poem. The eagle comes in like a gust of fresh air. The poem is suddenly alive. One of Chaucer's great comic characters has arrived on the scene.

The poet lies quiet in the eagle's grip for a space. Then his captor speaks—"in mannes vois," be it noted:

> Awak!
> And be not so a-gast, for shame!
> And called me tho by my name.
> And, for I sholde the bet abreyde—
> Me mette—'Awak,' to me he seyde,
> Right in the same vois, and stevene
> That useth oon I coude nevene.
>
> *Book* II, *ll.* 556–562

Chaucer takes heart, and composes himself to listen to what the eagle has to say. He must needs do this, for—as the delighted reader soon begins to realize—the eagle is a bore, the

first genuine, convincing bore in English fiction, with his
victim firmly in his grasp many thousands of feet above the
ground. There is no escape. The stream of learning begins to
flow, and at first Chaucer listens with interest, for the eagle
proceeds to quieten some of his most urgent doubts.

> I wol thee telle what I am,
> And whider thou shalt, and why I cam
> To done this, so that thou take
> Good herte, and not for fere quake.
> Book II, *ll*. 601–604

he says, and we now learn that as a reward for his long and
faithful labour in the service of love Chaucer is to be taken to
the House of Fame, where he will learn "mo wonder thinges"
of Love and his dominion than there are grains of corn in a
barn.

So far so good. But the eagle has hardly begun, and for the
next three hundred lines Chaucer is obliged to listen to a
discourse on the nature of sound, together with much else of a
like sort. He is informed that light things tend to fly upward,
and that heavy things, on the other hand, tend to fall down;
that rivers normally flow to the sea, and contain fish; that
speech is sound, and that sound is broken air; and so on, and
so on. The eagle, delighted with his victim's docility, has by
this time worked himself into a state of high satisfaction:

> 'A ha!' quod he, 'lo, so I can
> Lewedly to a lewed man
> Speke, and shewe him swiche skiles
> That he may shake hem by the biles,
> So palpable they shulden be.
> But tel me this, now I pray thee,
> How thinkth thee my conclusioun?
> Quod he. 'A good persuasioun,'
> Quod I, 'hit is; and lyk to be
> Right so as thou hast preved me.'
> Book II, *ll*. 865–874

But now they are flying over fields and plains, hills and mountains, soaring ever upward towards the Galaxy and the Milky

Way. These constellations give the eagle another idea, and he turns eagerly to the poet. "Wilt thou lere of sterres aught?" he asks, his eye kindling. But Chaucer has had enough:

> 'Nay, certeinly, 'quod I,' right naught;
> And why? for I am now to old.'

This ought to have been enough, but the eagle has no intention of accepting defeat so easily. He resumes his blandishments:

> 'Elles I wolde thee have told,'
> Quod he, 'the sterres names, lo,
> And al the hevenes signes to,
> And which they been.' 'No fors,' quod I.

But even this uncompromising reply leaves him undaunted. He tries yet again. "Surely," he asks, "you want to know where all the stars are that you read about in those poets of yours; Castor, Pollux, and so on?" Chaucer shakes his head: "No fors," he says, "hit is no nede"; and patiently, courteously, and firmly, he explains exactly why 'it does not matter.'

> 'I leve as wel, so god me spede,
> Hem that wryte of this matere,
> As though I knew hir places here;
> And eek they shynen here so brighte,
> Hit shulde shenden al my sighte,
> To loke on hem.'
> *Book* II, *ll.* 1012–1017

The eagle realizes at last that he has met his match. "That may wel be," he says, somewhat gloomily, and after that is silent for a while.

It is impossible to do justice in brief quotation to the brilliance and subtlety of this dialogue. Book II of the poem is a masterpiece of comic writing, and it is exhilarating to see Chaucer moving so easily among the humorous cut and thrust, which is as good in its way as anything in *The Canterbury Tales*.

Book III, therefore, is something of an anticlimax, and

though it is full of fine passages of descriptive writing—the castle on the mountain of ice, the Hall of Fame, Æolus and his dread trumpets, the house of twigs in the valley—passages as fine in their way as anything Chaucer ever did, we find ourselves missing the dramatic excitement of Book II, and we long to see the eagle again. He does, in fact, make another appearance towards the end, but he is only the shadow of his former self. Possibly Chaucer's unexpected firmness had abashed him somewhat. However this may be, the poem itself is unfinished. It comes to an abrupt end with the appearance of a mysterious "man of greet auctoritee," but who or what he was we shall never know. Nor are we likely to know why Chaucer decided to leave his poem in mid-air.

Perhaps the simplest explanation is also the best. And that is that he was tired of *The Hous of Fame*, and was anxious to try his hand at something else.

For a great deal of Book III is confused, however much we may admire the brilliance of isolated passages. Even Chaucer's skill and resource cannot save the inevitable catalogues from dullness, and the portrait of Fame is allegory gone slightly beyond itself. He had done this sort of thing once and for all. The allegory of *The Legend of Good Women* is in a different category altogether, gracious and charming, personal in tone, and full of the poet's joy in the varied beauty of the world.

THE LEGEND OF GOOD WOMEN

Chaucer never wrote anything more engaging than the Prologue to this unfinished collection of the lives of famous women faithful in love. And in it he entertains us by one of his rare excursions into autobiography, telling us of his love of books, of

> . . . these olde appreved stories,
> Of holinesse, of regnes, of victories,

> Of love, of hate, of other sundry thinges . . .
> And to hem yeve I feyth and ful credence,
> And in myn herte have hem in reverence.
> *Text B, ll.* 21–23; 31–32

The only thing, he says, which can drag him from their friendly presence is a longing, when May comes, to see the flowers shining in the sun; above all

> . . . these floures whyte and rede,
> Swiche as men callen daysies in our toun.

After one such day in the meadows he comes home and dreams his last dream, in which he is accused by the God of Love of "hindering" his subjects by translating such a poem as the *Roman de la Rose* (Jean de Meung's part of it, no doubt!) and writing an account of a lover so faithless as Criseyde. But Queen Alceste intercedes for him, declaring that he "niste what he seyde," and that in any case he was probably commanded by "som persone," and therefore had no choice in the matter. However, his fault is none the less plain, and he cannot avoid punishment, in spite of *The Boke of the Duchesse* and the story of Palamon and Arcite. His penance shall be to write a book of true lovers:

> . . . a glorious Legende
> Of Gode Wommen, maidenes and wyves,
> That weren trewe in lovinge al hir lyves,

and he is to begin with Cleopatra. Chaucer awakes, with this injunction still sounding in his ears, and sets about his task at once.

The stories which follow are not, on the whole, among his best work, in spite of some passages of great beauty. He seems to have exhausted his pleasure in the new theme by the composition of the Prologue—there are two complete versions of it extant—and to be working somewhat against the grain. Nor need we wonder at this. The Canterbury Pilgrims were even now crowding in upon him, and at their firm touch the

graceful shapes of allegory, the wraiths of legend, dissolved
and faded.

> . . . These our actors,
> As I foretold you, were all spirits, and
> Are melted into air, into thin air.

TROILUS AND CRISEYDE

Critics have long been accustomed to divide Chaucer's
poetic career, like Gaul, into three parts; and indeed this
division is by no means without point, provided it is not taken
too seriously or conceived of as something chronologically
exact. For it is perfectly true that he began by careful imitation
and adaptation of French models, as we have seen; that he then
came under the quickening influence of Dante, Petrarch,
and Boccaccio; and that in the end he was able to get along
comfortably enough without help from anyone, or anything
save his own native wits.

He made his first visit to Italy in November 1372, when he
went to Genoa to help in negotiating a commercial treaty with
the merchants of that city. He spent exactly 174 days out of
England, not perhaps a very long time to a man engaged on a
piece of important official business. We may, however,
cheerfully subscribe to the view that he must have been
greatly impressed, if not positively overwhelmed, by all he
saw and heard, and that he went about in a haze of delight,
revelling in the sunshine and the multifarious colours of the
Renaissance·

As Coulton put it:

For Goethe, the soul of Italy was in its pagan antiquity; but
Chaucer found there a living art and living literature, the noblest
in the then world. The great semicircle of houses standing upon
projecting arches round the harbour of Genoa, which survived
to be drawn by Ruskin in their decay, would at once strike a noble

note of contrast to the familiar wooden dwellings built over Thames shingle at home; everywhere he would find greater buildings and brighter colours than in our northern air. The pale ghosts of frescoes which we study so regretfully were then in their first freshness, with thousands more which have long since disappeared. Wherever he went, the cities were already building, or had newly built, the finest of the Gothic structures which adorn them still; and Chaucer must have passed through Pisa and Florence like a new Æneas among the rising glories of Carthage.[1]

It would be interesting to know whether he knew anything of Italian literature before he went to Genoa. It may reasonably be assumed that he had already learned some Italian—probably this was one of the reasons why he was sent—and it may be that he was now about to see, in all its fascinating reality, a country whose poetry he had in fact been enjoying for some time. It is at least possible that he brought back with him manuscripts of the *Divina Commedia*, the *Teseide*, and *Il Filostrato*, but this need not mean that this was the first time he had become aware of their existence.

Dante he could but revere from a distance, though he absorbed as much of his style as he could. Petrarch he admired greatly, though he found little to his purpose in his work. Boccaccio, however, was a writer after his own heart, and he read and reread the *Teseide* and the *Filostrato* as eagerly as, years before, he had spent absorbing days and nights in contemplation of the *Roman de la Rose*.[2]

Il Filostrato ("The One Prostrated by Love"), which Boccaccio wrote somewhere about 1330, is a most attractive and competent piece of work. Its author was a great craftsman: he knew exactly what he wanted to do, and he did it with supreme skill. Few, if any, have excelled him in the art of telling a story. He is never dull, and he never attempts more

---

[1] *Chaucer and his England* (Methuen, 1908), pp. 42–43.
[2] See T. R. Lounsbury, *Studies in Chaucer* (New York, 1892), Vol. II, pp. 223–249.

than he knows he can perform: herein we can perhaps detect one of his limitations. But his work is always perfectly rounded off; complete and final. There is never anything to add: the task has been performed to the letter. In the *Decameron*, for example, he sets out to tell a hundred tales. And a hundred tales are duly told. There are no loose ends. One can only marvel at his calm and easy mastery of his material. Chaucer, on the other hand, beginning *The Canterbury Tales*, has some notion of telling a hundred and twenty stories, at any rate for a start. It is true that he died before he could complete more than a sixth part of this task. But somehow we feel that it could never have come to an end.

Troilus and Criseyde, however, is another matter.[1] It has a beginning, a middle, and an end; and it is the greatest single artistic triumph of Chaucer's career. To this extent, at any rate, we can profitably compare it with *Il Filostrato*. But there is this important difference to be considered.

Boccaccio is always in control of the situation. Chaucer, carried away by sympathy for his creatures, finds himself in the end in something of an impasse. It might fairly be argued that his Criseyde would not—indeed, could not—have behaved as Boccaccio's story insists that she did behave. This charming, timid, and sensitive young woman, whose every feature

> Shewede wel, that men might in hir gesse
> Honour, estat, and wommanly noblesse,

carried away in spite of her fears[2] (and quite apart from the blandishments of Pandarus) by the engaging qualities and noble character of Troilus, is required to betray him in the end with the most cynical and brutal effrontery. Boccaccio's

[1] The story of Troilus and Cressida is essentially a medieval invention. Its first appearance is in the twelfth century *Roman de Troie* of Benoît de Sainte Maure. This was followed in 1287 by Guido delle Colonne's *Historia Trojana*. Boccaccio used both these sources for *Il Filostrato*. See R. K. Gordon, *The Story of Troilus* (Dent, 1934), pp. xi–xviii. Professor Gordon includes a translation of the *Filostrato*.

[2] See Kittredge, *Chaucer and his Poetry*, p. 132.

Griseida does all this with complete unconcern, and we see nothing in the least strange in such behaviour, for she is merely acting in accordance with her nature. But Chaucer has from the beginning watched over his Criseyde with tender care, has seen her gradually develop, revealing new graces at every turn, and is, one suspects, more than half in love with her himself before his poem is fairly at an end. Then comes the dreadful *dénouement*, and he is completely helpless. He is like a man who sees a gulf opening suddenly beneath his feet. Yet the one thing he could not do was to alter the story: that was sacrosanct. Lollius had said thus and thus, and so it must be. He does the best he can, but it is clear that his best seems to him but a poor thing:

> Ne me ne list this sely womman chyde
> Ferther than the story wol deyvse.
> Hir name, allas! is publisshed so wyde,
> That for hir gilt it oughte y-now suffyse
> And if I mighte excuse hir any wyse,
> For she so sory was for hir untrouthe,
> Y-wis, I wolde excuse hir yet for routhe.
> *Book* V, *ll.* 1093–1099

Troilus, on the other hand, is in many respects the typical courtly lover, and so, doughty warrior though he is, he must act in many things according to the accepted code. Modern readers sometimes find it difficult to reconcile his undoubted powers in the field with his sighs and tears. But for medieval readers this problem did not exist. And it is well for us to remember, for our part, that the modern view which holds that all display of masculine emotion is indecent is very modern indeed.

Troilus, however, is very much more than a piece of convention, and it is a tribute to Chaucer's art and insight that we are never allowed to forget that he is a man, and, what is more, a man in every way worthy of the love of such an exquisite person as Criseyde:

This Troilus sat on his baye stede,
Al armed, save his heed, ful richely,
And wounded was his hors, and gan to blede,
On whiche he rood a pas, ful softely;
But swich a knightly sighte, trewely,
As was on him, was nought, with-outen faile,
To loke on Mars, that god is of batayle.

So lyk a man of armes and a knight
He was to seen, fulfild of heigh prowesse;
For bothe he hadde a body and a might
To doon that thing, as wel as hardinesse;
And eek to seen him in his gere him dresse,
So fresh, so yong, so weldy semed he,
It was an heven up-on him for to see.

Book II, *ll.* 624–637

Still, for all the charm of Criseyde and the manliness of Troilus, it is Pandarus who sets the final seal on Chaucer's triumph. There was no precedent for him in *Il Filostrato*, where Pandaro is the cousin of Griseida, the boon companion of Troilo and his exact contemporary. In Chaucer's hands he emerges as Criseyde's uncle, middle-aged, yet not so old as to be incapable of feeling, on occasion, the pangs of despised love.

His character is not easy to define in a few words. Chaucer never again attempted anything quite so complex. He gives us a picture of a man who is worldly-wise but not cynical, humorous but not gross, easy-going but not vicious. Pandarus is genuinely fond of his two young people, and anxious that they shall be happy. He certainly enjoys intrigue for its own sake, but he justifies his final deception of Criseyde—of which he has the grace to be slightly ashamed—by his conviction that he is acting in the best interests of both parties. And his grief when all ends in ruin, and he realizes that he has sinned for no lasting purpose, is genuine and moving. For Criseyde has deceived him too.

> This Pandarus, that alle these thinges herde,
> And wiste wel he seyde a sooth of this,
> He nought a word ayein to him answerde;
> For sory of his frendes sorwe he is,
> And shamed, for his nece hath doon a-mis;
> And stant, astoned of these causes tweye,
> As stille as stoon; a word ne coude he seye.
> *Book* V, *ll.* 1723–1729

It is not without significance that more than once we find our thoughts turning to Shakespeare, and to Falstaff. Pandarus has little of Sir John's rumbustiousness and devastating comic equipment; but the ripeness is there, and it is this quality that Chaucer here introduces into English literature for the first time. The language of Pandarus—the conversations throughout the poem are a perfect example of that art which conceals itself—is a stimulating *mélange* of shrewd observation, affectionate badinage, and delight in the sheer joy of living. He is the ideal companion, sympathetic but never sentimental; helpful, but never domineering:

> Touching thy lettre, thou art wys y-nough,
> I woot thow nilt it digneliche endyte;
> As make it with thise argumentes tough;
> Ne scrivenish or craftily thou it wryte;
> Beblotte it with thy teres eek a lyte;
> And if thou wryte a goodly word al softe,
> Though it be good, reherce it not to ofte.
>
> For though the beste harpour upon lyve
> Wolde on the beste souned joly harpe
> That ever was, with all his fingres fyve,
> Touche ay o streng, or ay o werbul harpe,
> Were his nayles poynted never so sharpe,
> It shulde maken every wight to dulle,
> To here his glee, and of his strokes fulle.
> *Book* II, *ll.* 1023–1036

One cannot help feeling that Chaucer himself must have been something like this.

Matthew Arnold once observed, in a phrase which has become famous, that Chaucer lacked "high seriousness." What exactly he meant by this is not clear; perhaps no more than that Chaucer is not Dante. But one may legitimately wonder whether he had ever read *Troilus and Criseyde* carefully through all its five books, for the artless ease with which Chaucer tells his story is deceptive. The poem goes deep. Much of the poignancy of Book V, for example, is at times almost unbearable. "Hope deferred maketh the heart sick," is the text, and nowhere else in English will you find such a subtle, almost relentless, analysis of the slow hours as they pass, and no one comes. And—to jump for a moment across six centuries—there is no letter in the box.

There are few scenes in medieval literature more touching than the picture of true love satisfied in Book III: few passages of such sustained lyrical quality as the 'Trojan lay' sung by Antigone in Book II. The whole poem is full of surprises, but it yields up its beauties slowly, and they are best appreciated as they rise from time to time above the orderly and sustained march of the story.

Troilus and Criseyde is still the finest narrative poem in English, and in the broadcasts of Mr Nevill Coghill's modernized version we have been given the opportunity of observing that the years have but deepened and intensified the quality of its unique appeal.

THE CANTERBURY TALES

The modern critic of Chaucer, faced with the prospect of yet one more appraisal of *The Canterbury Tales*, is apt to be overcome by an acute sense of his inadequacy. "Tout est dit," said La Bruyère (though he was not thinking of Chaucer) ". . . l'on ne fait que glaner après les anciens et les habiles d'entre les modernes."

Yet, fortunately, this is not the whole story. It still remains.

D

true that every lover of poetry must find his poets for himself. In the last resort there is no substitute for the text—the *ipsissim averba*—of the author, whoever he may be. But where Chaucer is concerned that text will not come fully alive unless we take the trouble to look farther afield. He has something for every one, no doubt: God's plenty is not likely to prove insufficient, whatever demands are made upon it. But to know something—as much as we can, in fact—of Chaucer's world is to put a much keener edge on our enjoyment. For example, we can only see the point of his wit if we know exactly what it is he is laughing at, and why he is amused. And it is pleasant to be able to follow him into the byways as well as along the high road.

There are, then, two ways of reading Chaucer. The first is to take him as he comes, so to speak, and to base our enjoyment on that in him which is rooted in the universal, independent of time or place: to absorb the permanent and human quality of his art, without which all the rest is as nothing. And a very great deal can undoubtedly be gained by such an approach as this. But we shall be still more richly rewarded if we supplement our reading by diligent inquiry into the world of his time, by penetrating into the minds and hearts of his contemporaries, by familiarizing ourselves with the minutiæ of social custom and observance.

There is, after all, a sense in which no poet, however great, can step one foot beyond the boundaries of his own age. Shakespeare, whatever else he may be, is always an Elizabethan, Milton as surely a man of the seventeenth century. Chaucer was in many ways a typical product of the Middle Ages, and it is futile to attempt to deal with him as though he existed in a vacuum.

> Whan that Aprille with his shoures sote
> The droghte of Marche hath perced to the rote,
> And bathed every veyne in swich licour,
> Of which vertu engendred is the flour;

Whan Zephirus eek with his swete breeth
Inspired hath in every holt and heeth
The tendre croppes, and the yonge sonne
Hath in the Ram his halfe cours y-ronne,
And smale fowles maken melodye,
That slepen al the night with open yë,
(So priketh hem nature in hir corages):
Than longen folk to goon on pilgrimages
(And palmers for to seken straunge strondes)
To ferne halwes, couthe in sondry londes.

Prologue to *The Canterbury Tales*, *ll.* 1–14

It is difficult either to define or explain the perennial sense of excitement which these simple words and images convey to lovers of Chaucer. Read them as often as you will, or hear them read; the old fascination returns in all its pristine vigour.

It was indeed a fortunate hour in which a great poet arrived in time to use an English with the dew on it. A few years more, and it would have been too late. Were it not for Chaucer, we should never have known what the English of the Middle Ages was really capable of in the hands of a master. Chaucer preserved its vernal freshness for ever. In his verse "the silver dropes hanging on the leves" are hanging there still. We have had poets—though not more than one or two—as great, and we may still hope for others. But the *kind* of poetry Chaucer wrote has gone for ever, with the world which gave it life.

We do not know when he first thought of assembling his pilgrims at the Tabard—somewhere about 1386, perhaps. One or two of the stories he was to use—"The Knight's Tale," for example, and possibly "The Monk's Tale," to mention no others—he had had by him for some time in a more or less finished state. The idea of a pilgrimage may have come to him as a sudden access of inspiration, or it may have been the result of long and careful thought, a process of trial and error: we do not know. What is certain is that it was a stroke of true genius, and, like all strokes of genius, amazingly simple in outline—when once you have thought of it.

Some have attempted to deprive Chaucer of his credit by pointing to others who had contrived that a group of people should meet together and tell tales—Boccaccio, for example.[1] But there is no evidence that Chaucer knew even of the existence of the *Decameron*, and, in any case, the static and rigid quality of its setting is as far removed from the life and movement of the Canterbury pilgrimage as are Boccaccio's shadowy young men and women from the laughing crowd, "wel nyne and twenty in a companye," who gather in the courtyard of Harry Bailly's inn.

Chaucer's scheme, unlike Boccaccio's, is flexible, capable of infinite variety, and open to any contingency. Anything may happen to a company on the road: the travellers may contrive adventure from within, or they may experience it from without. Indeed, a journey of this kind is subject to all the uncertainties of life itself, as Bunyan was to remind us three hundred years later. But it is in the links which bind the tales together—the joints, as it were, of this flexible framework —that Chaucer's power of creating an illusion of real life is seen to its greatest advantage. These interludes, which are one of the chief glories of the work, afford him a superb opportunity of exploiting his remarkable dramatic gifts, and for displaying that mastery of conversational verse towards which he had been moving for so many years, and which is now seen in all its ripe perfection. In these short and lively scenes the pilgrims argue and discuss, quarrel and make up, express their personal feelings on a wide range of topics, and regale us with fragments of autobiography. Here too the majestic figure of Harry Bailly, prince of innkeepers, comes into full view,

---

[1] The Arabian *Thousand and One Nights* is perhaps the most famous of all such collections of tales, but there is no evidence that Chaucer made any use of it, or that he even knew of its existence. But he may just possibly have seen the collection of *novelle* made by Giovanni Sercambi (1347–1424). See Manly, *Canterbury Tales*, pp. 74–77, and Kittredge, *Chaucer and his Poetry*, pp. 147–150

somewhat to our surprise, and greatly to our delight. We had hardly been prepared for anything quite like this by the laconic, almost non-committal sketch of him in the Prologue.

It has sometimes been suggested that in selecting his "sondry folke" Chaucer's intention was to provide his readers with a complete picture of the medieval scene: to offer a cross-section, in effect, of the England of his day. But, putting aside for the moment Manly's intriguing theory that the whole poem is a kind of charade in which every pilgrim represents some one known to Chaucer and his friends,[1] it is easy to see that this is on the whole unlikely. For the very great are not there, nor are the very lowly. It may perhaps be said that the very great were not in the habit of travelling in such company, and that the very lowly could not have afforded to do so, even if they could have spared the time. To which one may reply that if Chaucer had wished to depict the whole of medieval society he would have found a scheme better suited to his purpose. And, almost certainly, we should all have been the poorer.[2]

The fact is that although he was familiar enough with the very great he either knew little of the real poor or had decided to leave them out of account. He never says much about them at any time, though we ought not to forget the charming portrait of the humble widow in "The Nun's Priest's Tale." It is Langland who is our authority here. He knew them because he was one of them, and could write about them because he was articulate, and they were not. There is no need to labour the point, but it is worth remembering that there were some aspects of life to which Chaucer, for all his humanity and insight, was all his life a stranger.

The pilgrims themselves are, broadly speaking, of three kinds. Some are idealized figures: types, if you will. Others are direct transcripts from life. A few are something of both.

---

[1] *Some New Light on Chaucer* (G. Bell, 1927), *passim*, and particularly pp. 70–76.
[2] But see Nevill Coghill, *op. cit.*, pp. 115–118.

The Knight, that most attractive of soldiers, is also the personification of chivalry; the Clerk, of learning and scholarship; the Parson, of godliness; the Plowman, of honest toil, perhaps. The Miller and the Summoner, on the other hand, are simply themselves—of the earth earthy, and alive to the very tips of their fingers.

Harry Bailly, too, is very much larger than any category. He is a living Englishman, drawn in the round, and with a life of his own about which the reader may argue and theorize to his heart's content:

> Whan ended was my tale of Melibee,
> And of Prudence and hir benignitee,
> Our hoste seyde, 'as I am faithful man,
> And by the precious *corpus Madrian*,
> I hadde lever than a barel ale
> That goode lief my wyf hadde herd this tale!
> For she nis no-thing of swich pacience
> As was this Melibeus wyf Prudence.
> By goddes bones! whan I bete my knaves,
> She bringth me forth the grete clobbed staves,
> And cryeth, "slee the dogges everichoon,
> And brek hem, bothe bak and every boon."
> And if that any neighebor of myne
> Wol nat in chirche to my wyf enclyne,
> Or be so hardy to hir to trespace,
> When she comth hoom, she rampeth in my face,
> And cryeth, "false coward, wreek thy wyf!
> By *corpus* bones! I wol have thy knyf,
> And thou shalt have my distaf and go spinne!"
> "The Monk's Prologue," *ll.* 1–19

Many of the pilgrims are of his stamp, though few, perhaps, of his quality. The proof of this comes when we find ourselves wishing we knew what happened to them all when they got to Canterbury, wondering what the journey back was like, and which one of them it was who sat down to a free supper on that final riotous evening.[1]

[1] The anonymous author of *The Tale of Beryn* did in fact attempt to continue the narrative as far as the beginning of the return journey. See Kittredge, *Chaucer and his Poetry*, pp. 156–157.

Chaucer's method of achieving these miracles of portraiture
—for they are nothing less—is disarmingly simple. Time is
short, so each character must be painted in quickly. Profession,
appearance, dress, and personal habits each receive a rapid and
penetrating glance, and the little portrait comes to life, as
vividly as if it had just been inserted at that moment into one of
the large initial letters of an illuminated manuscript.

Yet Chaucer is not always bound in by the claims of strict
relevancy. The Cook's "mormal," for instance, is such a
strange and unusual feature that here at any rate it is tempting
to agree with Manly that a real cook is sitting for his picture.
It is otherwise difficult to account for the connexion between
an ulcer and the making of the best blankmanger. Unless—
unless what we are dealing with is simply another manifestation
of that many-sided sense of humour which has so often led the
unsuspecting into strange places. There can be no doubt that
there are dangers lying in wait for the present-day reader who
wishes to extract all he can from the humour of Chaucer.
Sometimes the joke is obvious enough; too obvious, perhaps,
for our modern susceptibilities. At other times it is so tenuous
that we find ourselves wondering whether what we have before
us is a joke at all.

One thing, at any rate, ought to be remembered. It is easy—
fatally easy—to carry back into the Middle Ages our own
contemporary notions of what is amusing. Medieval manners
and speech—even medieval spelling—can assume for us an
aspect which was completely unknown to any reader of
Chaucer's day. At times like these the poet may come in
for a little unlooked-for credit, when in fact he is merely
behaving in normal medieval fashion. Chaucer would have
been the last person to complain if he had known that his work
might occasionally gain something from the mere passage of
time and the changing face of habit. It is, no doubt, a perfectly
legitimate form of pleasure which delights in the flavour of old
ways of speech and thought, provided always that we do not

make the disastrous—the fatal—mistake of laughing at Chaucer rather than with him. There indeed, if anywhere, pride goeth before a fall.

Some people, it must be admitted, distrust all humour, of whatever kind, and are prone to think that a humorous poet is a perfect example of a contradiction in terms. And Chaucer has sometimes been obliged to face the charge that, since he often found things to laugh at, he never thought very deeply about anything. His tolerance has been denigrated as indifference; his easy acceptance of the frankly sensual cited as evidence of a lack of moral fibre. There is, perhaps, just enough truth in some of these observations to give them a certain spurious attractiveness, and it has already been suggested that his view of the world was not Langland's. The only pilgrims he seems actively to dislike are the Pardoner and the Summoner, and even here cheerfulness will come breaking in. However, it is important, in a matter of this kind, to distinguish at once between thinking and writing. Chaucer's mind was as clear as that of any poet whatsoever, and if he can, for example, describe his Monk with merciless accuracy, listen to his preposterous arguments with patience, and then blandly and ironically observe, "And I seyde his opinioun was good," this is not because he cannot see what his remark may imply. The point is that here he is not only an author, but a member of the Canterbury pilgrimage, and in that capacity he wishes to avoid an unpleasant argument and to preserve harmony.

Moreover, it is never safe to forget that Chaucer—by training, at least—was an aristocrat. There were some subjects, he may well have thought, which were unsuitable for poetic treatment, some things which it was hardly proper for a man of his standing to get excited about. It was, in the last resort, a question of taste. One could hardly unload on a small circle of like-minded friends a series of tirades on the evils rampant in Church and State, however clearly one might be aware of them. A subtle and well-bred jest would serve one's purpose quite as well, and perhaps better. For all that, Chaucer's tolerance was real enough. His calm acceptance of things as they are is not a screen for secret wailings and gnashings of teeth.

The fact is that he enjoyed anything and everything which was good "in its kind." He was a connoisseur of essences, and that is why he remains unperturbed by some of his more disreputable characters. If they are fulfilling their rightful functions—and one of these is to amuse Geoffrey Chaucer, student of human nature—he can accept them cheerfully, spots and all. His curiosity was insatiable, and his capacity for enjoyment as great as his ability to convey it to others.

And he possessed, as we have seen, one indispensable piece of equipment: a power of self-detachment which enabled him to laugh, and laugh heartily, at himself. He is often amused, but he is rarely scornful; usually sympathetic; often both admiring and respectful. He does not take sides. He is content to enjoy the absorbing spectacle of mankind on the march, to paint his pictures as clearly as he can, and to leave his readers to do the rest.

The consequence is that there are some facets of his character which still remain in shadow. Do his hymns and prayers, the pious stories in *The Canterbury Tales*, prove that he was a deeply religious man? Perhaps. Many have not doubted it.[1] But the evidence is incomplete. And what of the epilogue to the Tales, that conclusion which strikes us at first sight with a feeling almost akin to horror?

Wherfore I biseke yow mekely for the mercy of god, that ye preye for me, that Crist have mercy on me and foryeve me my giltes:—and namely, of my translacions and endytinges of worldly vanitees, the whiche I revoke in my retracciouns: as is the book of Troilus; The book also of Fame; The book of the nynetene Ladies; The book of the Duchesse; The book of seint Valentynes day of the Parlement of Briddes; The tales of Caunterbury, thilke that sounen in-to sinne;

[1] The student should read, but with caution, G. K. Chesterton's *Chaucer* (Faber, 1948).

The book of the Leoun; and many another book, if they were in my remembrance; and many a song and many a lecherous lay; that Crist for his grete mercy foryeve me the sinne.

"The Parson's Tale," *ll.* 1007–1024

Can he, we ask ourselves, really mean all this? Is it possible that he was ashamed, at the last, of so much that we now prize so highly? The seemingly solid ground shifts a little under our feet. We may fortify ourselves by the reflection that Boccaccio similarly disavowed the *Decameron*, and murmur phrases about common form and normal contemporary practice. But we also remember Chaucer's often-repeated assurances that all is written for our instruction, his frequent anxiety to rebut a possible accusation of levity, or worse. We call to mind his elaborate apology for the less edifying parts of *The Canterbury Tales*. And we glimpse for a moment that other medieval world, where poetry is but a toy, a momentary and insignificant solace for children, and where those who have faith but not works shall utterly perish. And all at once we are a little uneasy.

The tales themselves are, as many generations have found, triumphs of technical skill, fascinating in their diversity of interest and appeal. As Mr H. S. Bennett observes:

Chaucer uses this variety of material to the utmost advantage, keeping his audience constantly uncertain of what next was in store for them. For example, the Wife of Bath's very worldly prologue is followed by her tale of the days of King Arthur, and when this is told the Friar's lewd tale follows and provokes one equally lewd from the Summoner. Then Chaucer (in the guise of Harry Bailly) firmly directs the Clerk to tell him "som murie thyng of aventures" which will not send them to sleep by its dullness, nor be couched in terms too difficult for them to understand. In the story of Griselda which follows, the Clerk provides an admirable contrast to the overwhelming 'masterie' of the Wife, or the earthy humours of the Friar and Summoner. The patience and devotion of Griselda are thrown into sharp contrast with the wifely behaviour of May as described by the next narrator—the Merchant. This done, the Squire's Tale provides an interlude of romance, and this is followed by the Franklin's narrative, with its mixture of magic, romance, and the supernatural. So throughout the *Canterbury Tales*—grave and gay, worldly, supernatural, or elemental—all have their turn and mingle together in our memory to make up the world that is the *Canterbury Tales*.[1]

Modern readers can sometimes be heard to complain that Chaucer too often refuses to get on with the story; they find themselves becoming slightly irritated by long addresses to the reader, disquisitions on this and that—when all they are anxious to know is what happened next. But these pauses and languors are no evidence of incapacity. Chaucer knew very well what he was doing, and for whom he was writing, and if he considers that the situation requires it he can tell his tale with a speed, economy, and directness which Boccaccio himself could not have bettered.[2] The tales of the Miller and the Reeve are evidence enough of this; so also are the central narratives of the Pardoner's tale and the tale of the Nun's Priest. These stories move without delay towards their inevitable end, but there is nothing bald or under-nourished about them. And what a variety of things are thrown in for good measure on the way!

For example, the larger canvas afforded by the tales (and the greater amount of time now at his disposal) gives him an opportunity of trying his hand at portrait-studies of a more elaborate kind than those of the Prologue. The most justly famous of these is his description of Alisoun, the heroine—if that is precisely the right word—of "The Miller's Tale." Here we can appreciate to the full Chaucer's pleasure in the concrete image, the homely and familiar analogy which penetrates at

[1] *Chaucer and the Fifteenth Century* (Oxford University Press, 1947) p. 73.
[2] "Most, if not all, of the so-called digressions in the Canterbury Tales are made by the teller of the story, not by the author. In other words, they are, in each case, a definite part of the dramatic plan; they grow out of the character or the situation." Kittredge, *op. cit.*, p. 25.

once to the heart of the matter: "things that we can touch and see," as the old Latin grammar used to say.

> Fair was this yonge wyf, and ther-with-al
> As any wesele hir body gent and smal.
> A ceynt she werede barred al of silk,
> A barmclooth eek as whyt as morne milk
> Up-on hir lendes, ful of many a gore.
> Whyt was hir smok, and brouded al bifore
> And eek bihinde, on hir coler aboute,
> Of col-blak silk, with-inne and eek with-oute,
> The tapes of hir whyte voluper
> Were of the same suyte of hir coler;
> Hir filet brood of silk, and set ful hye:
> And sikerly she hadde a likerous yë.
> Ful smale y-pulled were hir browes two,
> And tho were bent, and blake as any sloo.
> She was ful more blisful on to see
> Than is the newe pere-jonette tree;
> And softer than the wolle is of a wether.
> And by hir girdel heeng a purs of lether
> Tasseld with silk, and perled with latoun.
> In al this world, to seken up and doun,
> There nis no man so wys, that coude thenche
> So gay a popelote, or swich a wenche.
> Ful brighter was the shyning of hir hewe
> Than in the tour the noble y-forged newe.
> But of hir song, it was as loude and yerne
> As any swalwe sittinge on a berne.
> Ther-to she coude skippe and make game,
> As any kide or calf folwinge his dame.
> Hir mouth was swete as bragot or the meeth,
> Or hord of apples leyd in hey or heeth.
> Winsinge she was, as is a joly colt,
> Long as a mast, and upright as a bolt.
>
> "The Miller's Tale," *ll.* 47–78

It is a brilliant summary, but it is by no means the only thing of its kind, and the tales are full of proverbs, tags, jokes, allusions, and phrases which illuminate both characters and story like a flash of lightning. A lifetime of observation may be summed up in one unforgettable sentence; a whole world of experience displayed in an aside or a parenthesis. We see a master of both language and story-telling at the very height of his powers, handling his material with the careless and assured ease of a virtuoso. For all that, Chaucer never forgets the ends in the delight of conscious power over the means. He loves words for their own sake—the less poet he if he did not—but he never allows them to lead him either into obscurity or grandiloquence.

THE LEGACY OF CHAUCER'S POETRY

What then, finally, has Chaucer to offer us to-day, when poetry has come to mean, for most people, something very different from his leisurely and measured art? We shall look in vain for many things which have now become part of the heritage of all English-speaking peoples: the impassioned lyricism of a Shelley, the all-embracing wisdom of a Shakespeare. This is not the place for a detailed analysis of Chaucer's language, but consider for a moment how much of the Prologue alone has become part of even the smallest anthology of quotations:

> He was a verray parfit gentil knight.
>
> He was as fresh as is the month of May.
>
> Lat Austin have his swink to him reserved.
>
> And gladly wolde he lerne, and gladly teche.
>
> But Cristes lore, and his apostles twelve,
> He taughte, and first he folwed it himselve.

So one could go on. A perfection of phrase which can outlive six centuries is no indifferent legacy; and we cannot describe such triumphs better than by saying simply that they are Chaucerian. They ring with a note which is at once authentic and unique.

We have already seen that Chaucer's outward semblance is calm, almost sedate, and that he does not reveal himself in the modern way, sharing his private joys and sorrows with his readers. And it is precisely because this is so that we turn to him almost with a sense of relief after the burden and heat of other poets' days, for he is the least demanding and most companionable of men. It is soothing to be in the company of one who can be trusted to avoid hysteria even in the most disturbing of situations, who is widely read and pleasantly informative, whose comments on men and affairs are shrewd and kindly, whose generosity is deep and wide, whose sense of humour is unfailing.

Balance. Perhaps that, in the end, is the secret. Nothing too much. The right word, and the right feeling, in the right place. And all without rigidity or any sense of conscious rectitude. For Chaucer—one must say it yet once more—moves in a world which, for all its crudity and narrowness, was more equable and more spontaneous than our own. We know more than he ever dreamed of, and some of it has, perhaps, done us little good. We see a great deal farther than he could, and we notice a great deal less. Chaucer knows what is due to the dignity of mankind in general and himself in particular, and he is comfortable in his surroundings because the ultimate foundations of his world are sure. And when he writes he knows, beyond question, that he is on the true road. Ahead of him, in one long, unbroken procession, are the "auctors," the great ones: Virgil, Ovid, Dante, Petrarch, Deschamps, Machaut, Lollius—it is all one. For him there is no ancient or modern. He joins the rear of the line with characteristic modesty, yet with quiet confidence in his right to a place in that great company of the immortals.[1]

[1] Chaucer died on October 25, 1400. He was buried in Westminster Abbey, not because he was a poet—which seems strange to us now—but because the house he had leased on Christmas Eve, 1399, was the property of the Abbey, and as its tenant he had a right of burial in the precincts. It was not until 1556 that a monument was erected over his grave by Nicholas Brigham, an Elizabethan admirer.

THE CHIEF DATES IN CHAUCER'S LIFE

c. 1343. Born in London, to John and Agnes Chaucer.

1357. Page in the household of Elizabeth of Ulster, Duchess of Clarence.

1359–60. With the army in France. Taken prisoner, and ransomed with the aid of a contribution of £16 from Edward III.

1366 (?). Marries Philippa Roet.

1367. Yeoman in the King's household. Receives a pension of twenty marks for life.

1368. One of the Esquires of the Royal Household.

1369. With John of Gaunt and his army in Picardy.

1372. First visit to Italy.

1374. Controller of the customs on wool, hides, and sheepskins in the Port of London.

1375. Granted a daily pitcher of wine (commuted in 1387 to an additional pension of twenty marks).

Receives a pension of £10 from John of Gaunt.

Moves from Court to his house above Aldgate.

1376–77. Employed on diplomatic missions to France and Flanders.

1377. Accession of Richard II.

1378. Second visit to Italy.

1385. Justice of the Peace for Kent.

1386. Knight of the Shire (member of Parliament) for Kent.

1387 (?). Death of Philippa Chaucer.

1389–91. Clerk of the King's Works, including the Tower, Westminster Palace, and St George's Chapel, Windsor.

1391. Deputy Forester of the Royal Forest of North Petherton, in Somerset.

1393. Receives £10 as a gift from the King.

1394. Granted a new annuity of £20.

1397. Granted a butt of wine yearly.

1399. Accession of Henry IV. Granted an annuity of forty marks in addition to the £20 granted by Richard II.

Leases a house in the garden of Westminster Abbey.

1400. Dies, and is buried in the Abbey.

SELECTIONS FROM CHAUCER'S WORKS

SHORTER POEMS

To Rosemounde. A Balade

Madame, ye ben of al beautè shryne
As fer as cercled is the mappemounde;
For as the cristal glorious ye shyne,
And lyke ruby ben your chekes rounde.
Therwith ye ben so mery and so jocounde,
That at a revel whan that I see you daunce,
It is an oynement unto my wounde,
Thogh ye to me ne do no daliaunce.

For thogh I wepe of teres ful a tyne,
Yet may that wo myn herte nat confounde;   10
Your seemly voys that ye so smal out-twyne
Maketh my thoght in joye and blis habounde.
So curteisly I go, with lovë bounde,
That to my-self I sey, in my penaunce,
Suffyseth me to love you, Rosemounde,
Thogh ye to me ne do no daliaunce.

Nas never pyk walwed in galauntyne
As I in love am walwed and y-wounde;
For which ful ofte I of my-self divyne
That I am trewe Tristam the secounde.   20
My love may not refreyd be nor afounde;
I brenne ay in an amorous plesaunce.
Do what you list, I wil your thral be founde,
Thogh ye to me ne do no daliaunce.

Truth

BALADE DE BON CONSEYL

Flee fro the prees, and dwelle with sothfastnesse,
Suffyce unto thy good, though hit be smal;
For hord hath hate, and climbing tikelnesse,
Prees hath envye, and wele blent overal;
Savour no more than thee bihove shal;
Werk wel thy-self, that other folk canst rede;
And trouthe shal delivere, hit is no drede.

Tempest thee noght al croked to redresse,
In trust of hir that turneth as a bal:
Gret reste stant in litel besinesse;   10
And eek be war to sporne ageyn an al;
Stryve noght, as doth the crokke with the wal.
Daunte thy-self, that dauntest otheres dede;
And trouthe shal delivere, hit is no drede.

That thee is sent, receyve in buxumnesse,
The wrastling for this worlde axeth a fal.
Her nis non hoom, her nis but wildernesse:
Forth, pilgrim, forth! Forth, beste, out of thy stal!
Know thy contree, look up, thank God of al;
Hold the hye wey, and lat thy gost thee lede: 20
And trouthe shal delivere, hit is no drede.

ENVOY

Therfore, thou vache, leve thyn old wrecchednesse
Unto the worlde; leve now to be thral;
Crye him mercy, that of his hy goodnesse
Made thee of noght, and in especial
Draw unto him, and pray in general
For thee, and eek for other, hevenlich mede;
And trouthe shal delivere, hit is no drede.

E

Chaucers Wordes unto Adam, his Owne Scriveyn

Adam scriveyn, if ever it thee bifalle
Boece or Troilus to wryten newe,
Under thy lokkes thou most have the scalle,
But after my making thou wryte trewe.

So ofte a daye I mot thy werk renewe,
Hit to correcte and eek to rubbe and scrape;
And al is through thy negligence and rape.

FROM THE LONGER POEMS

The Romaunt of the Rose

THE DREAM

Within my twenty yere of age,
Whan that Love taketh his corage
Of yonge folk, I wente sone
To bedde, as I was wont to done,
And fast I sleep; and in sleping,
Me mette swiche a swevening,
That lykede me wonders wel;
But in that sweven is never a del
That it nis afterward befalle,
Right as this dreem wol telle us alle.   10
Now this dreem wol I ryme aright,
To make your hertes gaye and light;
For Love it prayeth, and also
Commaundeth me that it be so.
And if ther any aske me,
Whether that it be he or she,
How that this book the which is here
Shall hote, that I rede you here;
It is the Romance of the Rose,
In which al the art of love I close.   20

The mater fair is of to make;
God graunte in gree that she it take
For whom that it begonnen is!
And that is she that hath, y-wis,
So mochel prys; and ther-to she
So worthy is biloved be,
That she wel oughte, of prys and right,
Be cleped Rose of every wight.
   That it was May me thoughte tho,
It is fyve yere or more ago; 30
That it was May, thus dremed me,
In tyme of love and jolitee,
That al thing ginneth waxen gay,
For ther is neither busk nor hay
In May, that it nil shrouded been,
And it with newe leves wreen.
These wodes eek recoveren grene,
That drye in winter been to sene;
And th' erthe wexeth proud withalle,
For swote dewes that on it falle, 40
And al the pore estat forget
In which that winter hadde it set;
And than bicometh the ground so proud
That it wol have a newe shroud,
And maketh so queynt his robe and fayr
That it hath hewes an hundred payr
Of gras and floures, inde and pers,
And many hewes ful dyvers:
That is the robe I mene, y-wis,
Through which the ground to preisen is. 50
   The briddes, that han left hir song,
Whyl they han suffred cold so strong
In wedres grille, and derk to sighte,
Ben in May, for the sonne brighte,
So glade, that they shewe in singing,

That in hir herte is swich lyking,
That they mote singen and be light.
Than doth the nightingale hir might
To make noyse, and singen blythe.
Than is blisful, many a sythe,   60
The chelaundre and the papingay.
Than yonge folk entenden ay
For to ben gay and amorous,
The tyme is than so savorous.
Hard is his herte that loveth nought
In May, whan al this mirth is wrought;
Whan he may on these braunches here
The smale briddes singen clere
Hir blisful swete song pitous;
And in this sesoun delitous,   70
Whan love affrayeth alle thing,
Me thoughte a-night, in my sleping,
Right in my bed, ful redily,
That it was by the morowe erly,
And up I roos, and gan me clothe;
Anoon I wissh myn hondes bothe;
A sylvre nedle forth I drogh
Out of an aguiler queynt y-nogh,
And gan this nedle threde anon;
For out of toun me list to gon   80
The sowne of briddes for to here,
That on thise busshes singen clere.
And in the swete sesoun that leef is,
With a threde basting my slevis,
Aloon I wente in my playing,
The smale foules song harkning;
That peyned hem ful many a payre
To singe on bowes blosmed fayre.
Jolif and gay, ful of gladnesse,
Toward a river I gan me dresse,   90

That I herde renne faste by;
For fairer playing non saugh I
Than playen me by that riveer,
For from an hille that stood ther neer
Cam doun the streem ful stif and bold.
Cleer was the water, and as cold
As any welle is, sooth to seyne;
And somdel lasse it was than Seine,
But it was straighter wel away.
And never saugh I, er that day,   100
The water that so wel lyked me;
And wonder glad was I to see
That lusty place, and that riveer;
And with that water that ran so cleer
My face I wissh. Tho saugh I wel
The botme paved everydel
With gravel, ful of stones shene.
The medewe softe, swote, and grene,
Beet right on the water-syde.
Ful cleer was than the morow-tyde,   110
And ful attempre, out of drede.
Tho gan I walke through the mede,
Dounward ay in my pleying,
The river-syde costeying.

The Boke of the Duchesse

                    Ther was a king
That highte Seys, and hadde a wyf,
The beste that mighte bere lyf;
And this quene highte Alcyone.
So hit befel, therafter sone,
This king wolde wenden over see.
To tellen shortly, whan that he
Was in the see, thus in this wyse,

Soche a tempest gan to ryse
That brak hir mast, and made it falle,   10
And clefte hir ship, and dreinte hem alle,
That never was founden, as it telles,
Bord ne man, ne nothing elles.
Right thus this king Seys loste his lyf.
   Now for to speken of his wyf:—
This lady, that was left at home,
Hath wonder, that the king ne come
Hoom, for hit was a longe terme.
Anon her herte gan to erme;
And for that hir thoughte evermo   20
Hit was not wel he dwelte so,
She longed so after the king
That certes, hit were a pitous thing
To telle hir hertely sorwful lyf
That hadde, alas! this noble wyf;
For him she loved alderbest.
Anon she sente bothe eest and west
To seke him, but they founde nought.
   'Alas!' quoth she, 'that I was wrought!
And wher my lord, my love, be deed?   30
Certes, I nil never ete breed,
I make a-vowe to my god here,
But I mowe of my lorde here!'
Such sorwe this lady to her took
That trewely I, which made this book,
Had swich pite and swich rowthe
To rede hir sorwe, that, by my trowthe,
I ferde the worse al the morwe
After, to thenken on her sorwe.
   So whan she coude here no word   40
That no man mighte finde hir lord,
Ful oft she swouned, and seide 'alas!'
For sorwe ful nigh wood she was,

Ne she coude no reed but oon;
But doun on knees she sat anoon,
And weep, that pite was to here.
   'A! mercy! swete lady dere!'
Quod she to Juno, hir goddesse;
'Help me out of this distresse,
And yeve me grace my lord to see   50
Sone, or wite wher-so he be,
Or how he fareth, or in what wyse,
And I shal make you sacrifyse,
And hoolly youres become I shal
With good wil, body, herte, and al;
And but thou wilt this, lady swete,
Send me grace to slepe, and mete
In my slepe som certeyn sweven,
Wher-through that I may knowen even
Whether my lord be quik or deed.'   60
With that word she heng doun the heed,
And fil a-swown as cold as ston;
Hir women caughte her up anon,
And broghten hir in bed al naked,
And she, forweped and forwaked,
Was wery, and thus the dede sleep
Fil on her, or she toke keep,
Through Juno, that had herd hir bone,
That made hir for to slepe sone;
For as she prayde, so was don,   70
In dede; for Juno, right anon,
Called thus her messagere
To do her erande, and he com nere.
Whan he was come, she bade him thus:
'Go bet,' quod Juno, 'to Morpheus,
Thou knowest him wel, the god of sleep;
Now understond wel, and tak keep.
Sey thus on my halfe, that he

Go faste into the grete see,
And bid him that, on alle thing,   80
He take up Seys body the king,
That lyth ful pale and no-thing rody.
Bid him crepe into the body,
And do it goon to Alcyone
The quene, ther she lyth alone,
And shewe hir shortly, hit is no nay,
How hit was dreynt this other day;
And do the body speke so
Right as hit was wont to do,
The whyles that hit was on lyve.   90
Go now faste, and hy thee blyve!'
    This messager took leve and wente
Upon his wey, and never ne stente
Til he com to the derke valeye
That stant bytwene roches tweye,
Ther never yet grew corn ne gras,
Ne tree, ne nothing that ought was,
Beste, ne man, ne nothing elles,
Save ther were a fewe welles
Came renning fro the cliffes adoun,   100
That made a deedly sleping soun,
And ronnen doun right by a cave
That was under a rokke y-grave
Amid the valey, wonder depe.
Ther thise goddes laye and slepe,
Morpheus, and Eclympasteyre,
That was the god of slepes heyre,
That slepe and did non other werk.
    This cave was also as derk
As helle pit over-al aboute;   110
They had good leyser for to route
To envye, who might slepe beste;
Some henge hir chin upon hir breste

And slepe upright, hir heed y-hed,
And some laye naked in hir bed,
And slepe whyles the dayes laste.
    This messager com flying faste,
And cryed, 'O ho! awak anon!'
Hit was for noght; ther herde him non.
'Awak!' quod he, 'who is, lyth there?'   120
And blew his horn right in hir ere,
And cryed 'awaketh!' wonder hyë.
This god of slepe, with his oon yë
Cast up, axed, 'who clepeth there?'
'Hit am I,' quod this messagere;
'Juno bad thou shuldest goon'—
And tolde him what he shulde doon
As I have told yow here-tofore;
Hit is no need reherse hit more;
And wente his wey, whan he had sayd.   130
    Anon this god of slepe a-brayd
Out of his slepe, and gan to goon,
And did as he had bede him doon;
Took up the dreynte body sone,
And bar hit forth to Alcyone,
His wyf the quene, ther-as she lay,
Right even a quarter before day,
And stood right at hir beddes fete,
And called hir, right as she hete,
By name, and seyde, 'my swete wyf,   140
Awak! let be your sorwful lyf!
For in your sorwe ther lyth no reed;
For certes, swete, I nam but deed;
Ye shul me never on lyve y-see.
But good swete herte, look that ye
Bury my body, at whiche a tyde
Ye mowe hit finde the see besyde;
And far-wel, swete, my worldes blisse!

I praye god your sorwe lisse;
To litel whyl our blisse lasteth!' 150
    With that hir eyen up she casteth,
And saw noght; 'A!' quod she, 'for sorwe!'
And deyed within the thridde morwe.
But what she sayde more in that swow
I may not telle yow as now,
Hit were to longe for to dwelle;
My first matere I wil yow telle,
Wherfor I have told this thing
Of Alcione and Seys the king.

The Parlement of Foules

Nature, the vicaire of th'almyghty lorde,
That hoot, cold, hevy, light, and moist and dreye
Hath knit by even noumbre of acorde,
In esy vois began to speke and seye,
'Foules, tak hede of my sentence, I preye,
And, for your ese, in furthering of your nede,
As faste as I may speke, I wol me spede.

Ye know wel how, seynt Valentynes day,
By my statut and through my governaunce,
Ye come for to chese—and flee your way— 10
Your makes, as I prik yow with plesaunce.
But natheles, my rightful ordenaunce
May I not lete, for al this world to winne,
That he that most is worthy shal beginne.

The tercel egle, as that ye knowen wel,
The foul royal above yow in degree,
The wyse and worthy, secree, trewe as stel,
The which I formed have, as ye may see,
In every part as hit best lyketh me,

Hit nedeth noght his shap yow to devyse,   20
He shal first chese and speken in his gyse.

And after him, by order shul ye chese,
After your kinde, everich as yow lyketh,
And, as your hap is, shul ye winne or lese;
But which of yow that love most entryketh,
God sende him hir that sorest for him syketh.'
And therwith-al the tercel gan she calle,
And seyde, 'my sone, the choys is to thee falle.

But natheles, in this condicioun
Mot be the choys of everich that is here,   30
That she agree to his eleccioun,
Who-so he be that shulde been hir fere;
This is our usage alwey, fro yeer to yere;
And who so may at this time have his grace,
In blisful tyme he com in-to this place.'

With hed enclyned and with ful humble chere
This royal tercel spak and taried nought;
'Unto my sovereyn lady, and noght my fere,
I chese, and chese with wille and herte and thought,
The formel on your hond so wel y-wrought,   40
Whos I am al and ever wol hir serve,
Do what hir list, to do me live or sterve.

Beseching hir of mercy and of grace,
As she that is my lady sovereyne;
Or let me dye present in this place.
For certes, long may I not live in peyne;
For in myn herte is corven every veyne;
Having reward al only to my trouthe,
My dere herte, have on my wo som routhe.

And if that I to hir be founde untrewe,   50
Disobeysaunt, or wilful negligent,
Avauntour, or in process love a newe,
I pray to you this be my jugement,
That with these foules I be al to-rent,
That ilke day that ever she me finde
To hir untrewe, or in my gilte unkinde.

And sin that noon loveth hir so wel as I,
Al be she never of love me behette,
Than oghte she be myn thourgh hir mercy,
For other bond can I noon on hir knette.   60
For never, for no wo, ne shal I lette
To serven hir, how fer so that she wende;
Sey what yow list, my tale is at an ende.'

Right as the fresshe, rede rose newe
Ayen the somer-sonne coloured is,
Right so for shame al wexen gan the hewe
Of this formel, whan she herde al this;
She neyther answerde 'wel,' ne seyde amis,
So sore abasshed was she, til that Nature
Seyde, 'doghter, drede yow noght, I yow assure.'   70

Another tercel egle spak anoon
Of lower kinde, and seyde, 'that shal not be;
I love hir bet than ye do, by seynt John,
Or atte leste I love hir as wel as ye;
And lenger have served hir, in my degree,
And if she shulde have loved for long loving,
To me allone had been the guerdoning.

I dar eek seye, if she me finde fals,
Unkinde, jangler, or rebel any wyse,
Or jalous, do me hongen by the hals!   80

And but I bere me in hir servyse
As wel as that my wit can me suffyse,
Fro poynt to poynt, hir honour for to save,
Tak she my lyf, and al the good I have.'

The thridde tercel egle answerde tho,
'Now, sirs, ye seen the litel leyser here;
For every foul cryeth out to been a-go
Forth with his make, or with his lady dere;
And eek Nature hir-self ne wol nought here,
For tarying here, noght half that I wolde seye;   90
And but I speke, I mot for sorwe deye.

Of long servyse avaunte I me no-thing,
But as possible is me to dye to-day
For wo, as he that hath ben languisshing
Thise twenty winter, and wel happen may
A man may serven bet and more to pay
In half a yere, al-though hit were no more,
Than som man doth that hath served ful yore.

I ne say not this by me, for I ne can
Do no servyse that may my lady plese;   100
But I dar seyn, I am hir trewest man
As to my dome, and feynest wolde hir ese;
At shorte wordes, til that deth me sese,
I wol ben hires, whether I wake or winke,
And trewe in al that herte may bethinke.'

Of al my lyf, sin that day I was born,
So gentil plee in love or other thing
Ne herde never no man me beforn,
Who-so that hadde leyser and cunning
For to reherse hir chere and hir speking;   110
And from the morwe gan this speche laste
Til dounward drow the sonne wonder faste.

The noyse of foules for to ben delivered
So loude rong, 'have doon and let us wende!'
That wel wende I the wode had al toshivered.
'Come of!' they cryde, 'allas! ye wil us shende!
Whan shal your cursed pleding have an ende?
How shulde a juge eyther party leve,
For yee or nay, with-outen any preve?'

The goos, the cokkow, and the doke also   120
So cryden 'kek, kek!' 'kukkow!' 'quek, quek!' hye,
That thorgh myn eres the noyse wente tho.
The goos seyde, 'al this nis not worth a flye!
But I can shape hereof a remedye,
And I wol sey my verdit faire and swythe
For water-foul, who-so be wrooth or blythe.'

'And I for worm-foul,' seyde the fool cukkow,
'For I wol, of myn owne auctoritè,
For comune spede, take the charge now,
For to delivere us is gret charitè.'   130
'Ye may abyde a whyle yet, parde!'
Seide the turtel, 'if hit be your wille
A wight may speke, him were as good be stille.

I am a seed-foul, oon the unworthieste,
That wot I wel, and litel of kunninge;
But bet is that a wightes tonge reste
Than entremeten him of such doinge
Of which he neyther rede can nor singe.
And who-so doth, ful foule himself acloyeth,
For office uncommitted ofte anoyeth.'   140

Nature, which that alway had an ere
To murmour of the lewednes behinde,
With facound voys seide, 'hold your tonges there!

And I shal sone, I hope, a counseyl finde
You to delivere, and fro this noyse unbinde;
I juge, of every folk men shal oon calle
To seyn the verdit for you foules alle.'

Assented were to this conclusioun
The briddes alle; and foules of ravyne
Han chosen first, by pleyn eleccioun,   150
The tercelet of the faucon, to diffyne
Al hir sentence, and as him list, termyne;
And to Nature him gonnen to presente,
And she accepteth him with glad entente.

The tercelet seide than in this manere:
'Ful hard were hit to preve hit by resoun
Who loveth best this gentil formel here;
For everich hath swich replicacioun,
That noon by skilles may be broght a-doun;
I can not seen that arguments avayle;   160
Than semeth hit ther moste be batayle.'

'Al redy!' quod these egles tercels tho.
'Nay, sirs!' quod he, 'if that I dorste it seye,
Ye doon me wrong, my tale is not y-do!
For sirs, ne taketh noght a-gref, I preye,
It may noght gon, as ye wolde, in this weye;
Oure is the voys that han the charge in honde,
And to the juges dome ye moten stonde;

And therfor pees! I seye, as to my wit,
Me wolde thinke how that the worthieste   170
Of knighthode, and lengest hath used hit,
Moste of estat, of blode the gentileste,
Were sittingest for hir, if that hir leste;
And of these three she wot hir-self, I trowe,
Which that he be, for hit is light to knowe.'

The water-foules han her hedes leyd
Togeder, and of short avysement,
Whan everich had his large golee seyd,
They seyden sothly, al by oon assent,
How that 'the goos, with hir facounde gent,   180
That so desyreth to pronounce our nede,
Shal telle our tale,' and preyde 'god hir spede.'

And for these water-foules tho began
The goos to speke, and in hir cakelinge
She seyde, 'pees! now tak kepe every man,
And herkeneth which a reson I shal bringe;
My wit is sharp, I love no taryinge;
I seye, I rede him, though he were my brother,
But she wol love him, lat him love another!'

'Lo here! a parfit reson of a goos!'   190
Quod the sperhauk; 'never mot she thee!
Lo, swich hit is to have a tonge loos!
Now parde, fool, yet were hit bet for thee
Have holde thy pees, than shewed thy nycete!
Hit lyth not in his wit nor in his wille,
But sooth is seyd, "a fool can noght be stille."'

The laughter aroos of gentil foules alle,
And right anoon the seed-foul chosen hadde
The turtel trewe, and gunne hir to hem calle,
And preyden hir to seye the sothe sadde   200
Of this matere, and asked what she radde;
And she answerde, that pleynly hir entente
She wolde shewe, and sothly what she mente.

'Nay, god forbede a lover shulde chaunge!'
The turtel seyde, and wex for shame al reed;
'Thogh that his lady ever-more be straunge,

Yet let him serve hir ever, til he be deed;
For sothe, I preyse noght the gooses reed;
For thogh she deyed, I wolde non other make,
I wol ben hires, til that the deth me take.'   210

'Wel bourded!' quod the doke, 'by my hat!
That men shulde alwey loven, causeles,
Who can a reson finde or wit in that?
Daunceth he mury that is mirtheles?
Who shulde recche of that is recchelees?
Ye, quek!' yit quod the doke, ful wel and faire,
'There been mo sterres, god wot, than a paire!'

'Now fy, cherl!' quod the gentil tercelet,
'Out of the dunghil com that word ful right,
Thou canst noght see which thing is wel be-set: 220
Thou farest by love as oules doon by light,
The day hem blent, ful wel they see by night;
Thy kind is of so lowe a wrechednesse,
That what love is, thou canst nat see ne gesse.'

Tho gan the cukkow putte him forth in prees
For foul that eteth worm, and seide blyve,
'So I,' quod he, 'may have my make in pees,
I recche not how longe that ye stryve;
Lat ech of hem be soleyn al hir lyve,
This is my reed, sin they may not acorde;   230
This shorte lesson nedeth noght recorde.'

'Ye! have the glotoun fild ynogh his paunche,
Than are we wel!' seyde the merlioun;
'Thou mordrer of the heysugge on the braunche
That broghte thee forth, thou rewthelees glotoun!
Live thou soleyn, wormes corrupcioun!
For no fors is of lakke of thy nature;
Go, lewed be thou, whyl the world may dure!'

F

'Now pees,' quod Nature, 'I comaunde here;
For I have herd al your opinioun,   240
And in effect yet be we never the nere;
But fynally, this is my conclusioun,
That she hir-self shal han the eleccioun
Of whom hir list, who-so be wrooth or blythe,
Him that she cheest, he shal hir have as swythe.

The Hous of Fame

This egle, of which I have yow told,
That shoon with fethres as of gold,
Which that so hyë gan to sore,
I gan beholde more and more,
To see hir beautee and the wonder;
But never was ther dint of thonder,
Ne that thing that men calle foudre,
That smoot somtyme a tour to poudre,
And in his swifte coming brende,
That so swythe gan descende,   10
As this foul, whan hit behelde
That I a-roume was in the felde;
And with his grimme pawes stronge,
Within his sharpe nayles longe,
Me, fleinge, at a swappe he hente,
And with his sours agayn up wente,
Me caryinge in his clawes starke
As lightly as I were a larke,
How high, I can not telle yow,
For I cam up, I niste how.   20
For so astonied and a-sweved
Was every vertu in my heved,
What with his sours and with my drede,
That al my feling gan to dede;
For-why hit was to greet affray.
Thus I longe in his clawes lay,

Til at the laste he to me spak
In mannes vois, and seyde, 'Awak!
And be not so a-gast, for shame!'
And called me tho by my name. 30
And, for I sholde the bet abreyde—
Me mette—'Awak,' to me he seyde,
Right in the same vois and stevene
That useth oon I coude nevene;
And with that vois, soth for to sayn,
My minde cam to me agayn;
For hit was goodly seyd to me,
So nas hit never wont to be.

And herwithal I gan to stere,
And he me in his feet to bere, 40
Til that he felte that I had hete,
And felte eek tho myn herte bete.
And tho gan he me to disporte,
And with wordes to comforte,
And sayde twyës, 'Seynte Marie!
Thou art noyous for to carie,
And nothing nedeth hit, pardee!
For al-so wis god helpe me
As thou non harm shalt have of this;
And this cas, that betid thee is, 50
Is for thy lore and for thy prow;—
Let see! darst thou yet loke now?
Be ful assured, boldely,
I am thy frend.' And therwith I
Gan for to wondren in my minde.
'O god,' thoughte I, 'that madest kinde,
Shal I non other weyes dye?
Wher Joves wol me stellifye,
Or what thing may this signifye?
I neither am Enok, ne Elye, 60
Ne Romulus, ne Ganymede

That was y-bore up, as men rede,
To hevene with dan Jupiter,
And maad the goddes boteler.'
    Lo! this was tho my fantasye!
But he that bar me gan espye
That I so thoghte, and seyde this:—
'Thou demest of thy-self amis;
For Joves is not ther-aboute—
I dar wel putte thee out of doute—   70
To make of thee as yet a sterre.
But er I bere thee moche ferre,
I wol thee telle what I am,
And whider thou shalt, and why I cam
To done this, so that thou take
Good herte, and not for fere quake.'
'Gladly,' quod I. 'Now wel,' quod he:—
'First I, that in my feet have thee,
Of which thou hast a feer and wonder,
Am dwelling with the god of thonder,   80
Which that men callen Jupiter,
That dooth me flee ful ofte fer
To do al his comaundement.
And for this cause he hath me sent
To thee: now herkne, by thy trouthe!
Certeyn, he hath of thee routhe,
That thou so longe trewely
Hast served so ententifly
His blinde nevew Cupido,
And fair Venus goddesse also,   90
Withoute guerdoun ever yit,
And nevertheles hast set thy wit—
Although that in thy hede ful lyte is—
To make bokes, songes, dytees,
In ryme, or elles in cadence,
As thou best canst, in reverence

Of Love, and of his servants eke,
That have his servise soght, and seke;
And peynest thee to preyse his art,
Althogh thou haddest never part;   100
Wherfor, al-so god me blesse,
Joves halt hit greet humblesse
And vertu eek, that thou wolt make
A-night ful ofte thyn heed to ake,
In thy studie so thou wrytest,
And ever-mo of love endytest,
In honour of him and preysinges,
And in his folkes furtheringes,
And in hir matere al devysest,
And noght him nor his folk despysest,   110
Although thou mayst go in the daunce
Of hem that him list not avaunce.
    Wherfor, as I seyde, y-wis,
Jupiter considereth this,
And also, beau sir, other thinges;
That is, that thou hast no tydinges
Of Loves folk, if they be glade,
Ne of noght elles that god made;
And noght only fro fer contree
That ther no tyding comth to thee,   120
But of thy verray neyghebores,
That dwellen almost at thy dores,
Thou herest neither that ne this;
For whan thy labour doon al is,
And hast y-maad thy rekeninges,
In stede of reste and newe thinges,
Thou gost hoom to thy hous anoon;
And, also domb as any stoon,
Thou sittest at another boke,   130
Til fully daswed is thy loke,
And livest thus as an hermyte,
Although thyn abstinence is lyte.

Troilus and Criseyde

TROILUS SEES CRISEYDE FOR THE FIRST TIME

This Troilus, as he was wont to gyde
His yonge knightes, ladde hem up and doun
In thilke large temple on every syde,
Biholding ay the ladyes of the toun,
Now here, now there, for no devocioun
Hadde he to noon, to reven him his reste,
But gan to preyse and lakken whom him leste.

And in his walk ful fast he gan to wayten
If knight or squyer of his companye
Gan for to syke, or lete his eyen bayten   10
On any woman that he coude aspye;
He wolde smyle, and holden it folye,
And seye him thus, 'god wot, she slepeth softe
For love of thee, whan thou tornest ful ofte!

'I have herd told, pardieux, of your livinge,
Ye lovers, and your lewede observaunces,
And which a labour folk han in winninge
Of love, and, in the keping, which doutaunces;
And whan your preye is lost, wo and penaunces;
O verrey foles! nyce and blinde be ye;   20
Ther nis not oon can war by other be.'

And with that word he gan cast up the browe,
Ascaunces, 'lo! is this nought wysly spoken?'
At which the god of love gan loken rowe
Right for despyt, and shoop for to ben wroken;
He kidde anoon his bowe nas not broken;
For sodeynly he hit him at the fulle;
And yet as proud a pekok can he pulle.

O blinde world, O blinde entencioun!
How ofte falleth al th'effect contraire   30

Of surquidrye and foul presumpcioun;
For caught is proud, and caught is debonaire.
This Troilus is clomben on the staire,
And litel weneth that he moot descenden.
But al-day fayleth thing that foles wenden.

As proude Bayard ginneth for to skippe
Out of the wey, so priketh him his corn,
Til he a lash have of the longe whippe,
Than thenketh he, 'though I praunce al biforn
First in the trays, ful fat and newe shorn,   40
Yet am I but an hors, and horses lawe
I moot endure, and with my feres drawe.'

So ferde it by this fers and proude knight;
Though he a worthy kinges sone were,
And wende no-thing hadde had swiche might
Ayens his wil that sholde his herte stere,
Yet with a look his herte wex a-fere,
That he, that now was most in pryde above,
Wex sodeynly most subget un-to love.

For-thy ensample taketh of this man,   50
Ye wyse, proude, and worthy folkes alle,
To scornen Love, which that so sone can
The freedom of your hertes to him thralle;
For ever it was, and ever it shal bifalle,
That Love is he that alle thing may binde;
For may no man for-do the lawe of kinde.

That this be sooth, hath preved and doth yit;
For this trowe I ye knowen, alle or some,
Men reden not that folk han gretter wit
Than they that han be most with love y-nome;   60
And strengest folk ben therwith overcome,

The worthiest and grettest of degree;
This was, and is, and yet men shal it see.

And trewelich it sit wel to be so;
For alderwysest han ther-with ben plesed;
And they that han ben aldermost in wo,
With love han been conforted most and esed;
And ofte it hath the cruel herte apesed,
And worthy folk maad worthier of name,
And causeth most to dreden vyce and shame.   70

Now sith it may not goodly be withstonde,
And is a thing so vertuous in kinde,
Refuseth not to Love for to be bonde,
Sin, as him-selven list, he may yow binde.
The yerde is bet that bowen wole and winde
Than that that brest; and therfor I yow rede
To folwen him that so wel can yow lede.

But for to tellen forth in special
As of this kinges sone of which I tolde,
And leten other thing collateral,   80
Of him thenke I my tale for to holde,
Bothe of his joye, and of his cares colde;
And al his werk, as touching this matere,
For I it gan, I wil ther-to refere.

With-inne the temple he wente him forth pleyinge,
This Troilus, of every wight aboute,
On this lady and now on that lokinge,
Wher-so she were of toune, or of withoute:
And up-on cas bifel, that thorugh a route
His eye perced, and so depe it wente,   90
Til on Criseyde it smoot, and ther it stente.

And sodeynly he wex ther-with astoned,
And gan hire bet biholde in thrifty wyse:
'O mercy, god!' thoughte he, 'wher hastow woned,
That art so fair and goodly to devyse?'
Ther-with his herte gan to sprede and ryse,
And softe sighed, lest men mighte him here,
And caughte a-yein his firste pleyinge chere.

.   .   .   .   .

PANDARUS PAYS CRISEYDE A VISIT

In May, that moder is of monthes glade,
That fresshe floures, blewe, and whyte, and rede,
Ben quike agayn, that winter dede made,
And ful of bawme is fletinge every mede;
Whan Phebus doth his brighte bemes sprede
Right in the whyte Bole, it so bitidde
As I shal singe, on Mayes day the thridde,

That Pandarus, for al his wyse speche,
Felte eek his part of loves shottes kene,
That, coude he never so wel of loving preche,   10
It made his hewe a-day ful ofte grene;
So shoop it, that him fil that day a tene
In love, for which in wo to bedde he wente,
And made, er it was day, ful many a wente.

The swalwe Proignè, with a sorwful lay,
Whan morwe com, gan make hir weymentinge,
Why she forshapen was; and ever lay
Pandare a-bedde, half in a slomeringe,
Til she so neigh him made hir chiteringe
How Tereus gan forth hir suster take,   20
That with the noyse of hir he gan a-wake;

And gan to calle, and dresse him up to ryse,
Remembringe him his erand was to done
From Troilus, and eek his greet empryse;
And caste and knew in good plyt was the mone
To doon viage, and took his wey ful sone
Un-to his neces paleys ther bi-syde;
Now Janus, god of entree, thou him gyde!

Whan he was come un-to his neces place,
'Wher is my lady?' to hir folk seyde he;   30
And they him tolde; and he forth in gan pace,
And fond, two othere ladyes sete and she
With-inne a paved parlour; and they three
Herden a mayden reden hem the geste
Of the Sege of Thebes, whyl hem leste.

Quod Pandarus, 'madame, god yow see,
With al your book and al the companye!'
'Ey, uncle myn, welcome y-wis,' quod she,
And up she roos, and by the hond in hye
She took him faste, and seyde, 'this night thrye,   40
To goode mote it turne, of yow I mette!'
And with that word she doun on bench him sette.

'Ye, nece, ye shal fare wel the bet,
If god wole, al this yeer,' quod Pandarus;
'But I am sory that I have yow let
To herknen of your book ye preysen thus;
For goddes love, what seith it? tel it us.
Is it of love? O, som good ye me lere!"
'Uncle,' quod she, 'your maistresse is not here!'

With that they gonnen laughe, and tho she seyde,   50
'This romaunce is of Thebes, that we rede;
And we han herd how that king Laius deyde

Thurgh Edippus his sone, and al that dede;
And here we stenten at these lettres rede,
How the bisshop, as the book can telle,
Amphiorax, fil thurgh the ground to helle.'

Quod Pandarus, 'al this knowe I myselve,
And al th'assege of Thebes and the care;
For her-of been ther maked bokes twelve:—
But lat be this, and tel me how ye fare;   60
Do wey your barbe, and shew your face bare;
Do wey your book, rys up, and lat us daunce,
And lat us don to May som observaunce.'

'A! god forbede!' quod she, 'be ye mad?
Is that a widewes lyf, so god you save?
By god, ye maken me right sore a-drad,
Ye ben so wilde, it semeth as ye rave!
It sete me wel bet ay in a cave
To bidde, and rede on holy seyntes lyves:
Lat maydens gon to daunce, and yonge wyves.'   70

'As ever thryve I,' quod this Pandarus,
'Yet coude I telle a thing to doon you pleye.'
'Now uncle dere,' quod she, 'tel it us
For goddes love; is than th'assege aweye?
I am of Grekes so ferd that I deye.'
'Nay, nay,' quod he, 'as ever mote I thryve!
It is a thing wel bet than swiche fyve.'

'Ye, holy god!' quod she, 'what thing is that?
What? bet than swiche fyve? ey, nay, y-wis!
For al this world ne can I reden what   80
It sholde been; som jape, I trowe, is this;
And but your-selven telle us what it is,
My wit is for to arede it al to lene;
As help me god, I noot nat what ye mene.'

'And I your borow, ne never shal, for me,
This thing be told to yow, as mote I thryve!'
'And why so, uncle myn? why so?' quod she.
'By god,' quod he, 'that wole I telle as blyve;
For prouder womman were ther noon on-lyve,
And ye it wiste, in al the toun of Troye;   90
I jape nought, as ever have I joye!'

Tho gan she wondren more than biforn
A thousand fold, and doun hir eyen caste;
For never, sith the tyme that she was born,
To knowe thing desired she so faste;
And with a syk she seyde him at the laste,
'Now, uncle myn, I nil yow nought displese,
Nor axen more, that may do yow disese.'

．　．　．　．　．

Antigone's Song

Adoun the steyre anoon-right tho she wente
In-to the gardin, with hir neces three,
And up and doun ther made many a wente,
Flexippe, she, Tharbe, and Antigone,
To pleyen, that it joye was to see;
And othere of hir wommen, a gret route,
Hir folwede in the gardin al aboute.

This yerd was large, and rayled alle the aleyes,
And shadwed wel with blosmy bowes grene,
And benched newe, and sonded alle the weyes,   10
In which she walketh arm in arm bitwene;
Til at laste the Antigone the shene
Gan on a Trojan song to singe clere,
That it an heven was hir voys to here.—

She seyde, 'O love, to whom I have and shal
Ben humble subgit, trewe in myn entente,
As I best can, to yow, lord, yeve ich al
For ever-more, myn hertes lust to rente.
For never yet thy grace no wight sente
So blisful cause as me, my lyf to lede   20
In alle joye and seurtee, out of drede.

Ye, blisful god, han me so wel beset
In love, y-wis, that al that bereth lyf
Imaginen ne cowde how to ben bet;
For, lord, with-outen jalousye or stryf,
I love oon which that is most ententyf
To serven wel, unwery or unfeyned,
That ever was, and leest with harm distreyned.

As he that is the welle of worthinesse,
Of trouthe ground, mirour of goodliheed,   30
Of wit Appollo, stoon of sikernesse,
Of vertu rote, of lust findere and heed,
Thurgh which is alle sorwe fro me deed,
Y-wis, I love him best, so doth he me;
Now good thrift have he, wher-so that he be!

Whom sholde I thanke but yow, god of love,
Of al this blisse, in which to bathe I ginne?
And thanked be ye, lord, for that I love!
This is the righte lyf that I am inne,
To flemen alle manere vyce and sinne: 40
This doth me so to vertu for to entende,
That day by day I in my wil amende.

And who-so seyth that for to love is vyce,
Or thraldom, though he fele in it distresse,
He outher is envyous, or right nyce,

Or is unmighty, for his shrewednesse,
To loven; for swich maner folk, I gesse,
Defamen love, as no-thing of him knowe;
They speken, but they bente never his bowe.

What is the sonne wers, of kinde righte,   50
Though that a man, for feblesse of his yën,
May nought endure on it to see for brighte?
Or love the wers, though wrecches on it cryen?
No wele is worth, that may no sorwe dryen.
And for-thy, who that hath an heed of verre,
Fro cast of stones war him in the werre!

But I with al myn herte and al my might,
As I have seyd, wol love, un-to my laste,
My dere herte, and al myn owene knight,
In which myn herte growen is so faste,   60
And his in me, that it shal ever laste.
Al dredde I first to love him to biginne,
Now woot I wel, ther is no peril inne.'

And of hir song right with that word she stente,
And therwith-al, 'now, nece,' quod Criseyde,
'Who made this song with so good entente?'
Antigone answerde anoon, and seyde,
'Ma dame, y-wis, the goodlieste mayde
Of greet estat in al the toun of Troye;
And let hir lyf in most honour and joye.'   70

'Forsothe, so it semeth by hir song,'
Quod tho Criseyde, and gan ther-with to syke,
And seyde, 'lord, is there swich blisse among
These lovers, as they conne faire endyte?'
'Ye, wis,' quod fresh Antigone the whyte;
'For alle the folk that han or been on lyve
Ne conne wel the blisse of love discryve.

But wene ye that every wrecche woot
The parfit blisse of love? why, nay, y-wis;
They wenen al be love, if oon be hoot;   80
Do wey, do wey, they woot no-thing of this!
Men mosten axe at seyntes if it is
Aught fair in hevene; why? for they conne telle;
And axen fendes, is it foul in helle.'

Criseyde un-to that purpos nought answerde,
But seyde, 'y-wis, it wol be night as faste.'
But every word which that she of hir herde,
She gan to prenten in hir herte faste;
And ay gan love hir lasse for to agaste
Than it dide erst, and sinken in hir herte,   90
That she wex somewhat able to converte.

The dayes honour, and the hevenes yë,
The nightes fo, al this clepe I the sonne,
Gan westren faste, and dounward for to wrye,
As he that hadde his dayes cours y-ronne;
And whyte thinges wexen dimme and donne
For lak of light, and sterres for to appere,
That she and al hir folk in wente y-fere.

So whan it lyked hir to goon to reste,
And voyded weren they that voyden oughte,   100
She seyde, that to slepe wel hir leste.
Hir wommen sone til hir bed hir broughte.
Whan al was hust, than lay she stille, and thoughte
Of al this thing the manere and the wyse.
Reherce it nedeth nought, for ye ben wyse.

A nightingale, upon a cedre grene,
Under the chambre-wal ther as she lay,
Ful loude sang ayein the mone shene,

Paraunter, in his briddes wyse, a lay
Of love, that made hir herte fresh and gay.   110
That herkned she so longe in good entente.
Til at the laste the dede sleep hir hente.

. . . . . .

TROILUS LAMENTS THE LOSS OF HIS FORMER HAPPINESS

On morwe, as sone as day bigan to clere,
This Troilus gan of his sleep t'abreyde,
And to Pandare, his owene brother dere,
'For love of god,' ful pitously he seyde,
'As go we seen the paleys of Criseyde;
For sin we yet may have namore feste,
So lat us seen hir paleys at the leste.'

And ther-with-al, his meynee for to blende,
A cause he fond in toune for to go,
And to Criseydes hous they gonnen wende.   10
But lord! this sely Troilus was wo!
Him thoughte his sorweful herte braste a-two.
For whan he saugh hir dores sperred alle,
Wel neigh for sorwe a-doun he gan to falle.

Therwith whan he was war and gan biholde
How shet was every windowe of the place,
As frost, him thoughte, his herte gan to colde;
For which with chaunged deedlich pale face,
With-outen word, he forth bigan to pace;
And, as god wolde, he gan so faste ryde,   20
That no wight of his contenaunce aspyde.

Than seyde he thus, 'O paleys desolat,
O hous, of houses whylom best y-hight,
O paleys empty and disconsolat,

O thou lanterne, of which queynt is the light,
O paleys, whylom day, that now art night,
Wel oughtestow to falle, and I to dye,
Sin she is went that wont was us to gye!

O paleys, whylom croune of houses alle,
Enlumined with sonne of alle blisse!
O ring, fro which the ruby is out-falle,
O cause of wo, that cause hast been of lisse!
Yet, sin I may no bet, fayn wolde I kisse
Thy colde dores, dorste I for this route;
And fare-wel shryne, of which the seynt is oute!'

Ther-with he caste on Pandarus his yë
With chaunged face, and pitous to biholde;
And whan he mighte his tyme aright aspye,
Ay as he rood, to Pandarus he tolde
His newe sorwe, and eek his joyes olde,
So pitously and with so dede an hewe,
That every wight mighte on his sorwe rewe.

Fro thennesforth he rydeth up and doun,
And every thing com him to remembraunce
As he rood forth by places of the toun
In whiche he whylom hadde al his plesaunce.
'Lo, yond saugh I myn owene lady daunce;
And in that temple, with hir eyen clere,
Me caughte first my righte lady dere.

And yonder have I herd ful lustily
My dere herte laughe, and yonder pleye
Saugh I hir ones eek ful blisfully.
And yonder ones to me gan she seye,
"Now goode swete, love me wel, I preye."
And yond so goodly gan she me biholde,
That to the deeth myn herte is to hir holde.

G

And at that corner, in the yonder hous,
Herde I myn alderlevest lady dere
So wommanly, with voys melodious,
Singen so wel, so goodly, and so clere,   60
That in my soule yet me thinketh I here
The blisful soun; and, in that yonder place,
My lady first me took un-to hir grace.'

Thanne thoughte he thus, 'O blisful lord Cupyde,
Whanne I the proces have in my memorie,
How thou me hast werreyed on every syde,
Men mighte a book make of it, lyk a storie.
What nede is thee to seke on me victorie,
Sin I am thyn, and hoolly at thy wille?
What joye hastow thyn owene folk to spille?   70

Wel hastow, lord, y-wroke on me thyn ire,
Thou mighty god, and dredful for to greve!
Now mercy, lord, thou wost wel I desire
Thy grace most, of alle lustes leve.
And live and deye I wol in thy bileve;
For which I n'axe in guerdon but a bone,
That thou Criseyde ayein me sende sone.

Distreyne hir herte as faste to retorne
As thou dost myn to longen hir to see;
Than woot I wel, that she nil not sojorne.   80
Now, blisful lord, so cruel thou ne be
Un-to the blood of Troye, I preye thee,
As Juno was un-to the blood Thebane,
For which the folk of Thebes caughte hir bane.'

And after this he to the yates wente
Ther-as Criseyde out-rood a ful good paas,
And up and doun ther made he many a wente,

And to him-self ful ofte he seyde 'allas!
From hennes rood my blisse and my solas!
As wolde blisful god now, for his joye,   90
I mighte hir seen ayein come in-to Troye.

And to the yonder hille I gan hir gyde,
Allas! and there I took of hir my leve!
And yond I saugh hir to hir fader ryde,
For sorwe of which myn herte shal to-cleve.
And hider hoom I com whan it was eve;
And here I dwelle out-cast from alle joye,
And shal, til I may seen hir eft in Troye.'

     . . . . .

The End of the Story

In many cruel batayle, out of drede,
Of Troilus, this ilke noble knight,
As men may in these olde bokes rede,
Was sene his knighthod and his grete might.
And dredelees, his ire, day and night,
Ful cruelly the Grekes ay aboughte;
And alwey most this Diomede he soughte.

And ofte tyme, I finde that they mette
With blody strokes and with wordes grete,
Assayinge how hir speres weren whette;   10
And god it woot, with many a cruel hete
Gan Troilus upon his helm to-bete.
But natheless, fortune it nought ne wolde,
Of otheres hond that either deyen sholde.—

And if I hadde y-taken for to wryte
The armes of this ilke worthy man,
Than wolde I of his batailles endyte.

But for that I to wryte first bigan
Of his love, I have seyd as that I can.
His worthy dedes, who-so list hem here,   20
Reed Dares, he can telle hem alle y-fere.

Bisechinge every lady bright of hewe,
And every gentil womman, what she be,
That al be that Criseyde was untrewe,
That for that gilt she be not wrooth with me.
Ye may hir gilt in othere bokes see;
And gladlier I wol wryten, if yow leste,
Penelopeës trouthe and good Alceste.

Ne I sey not this al-only for these men,
But most for wommen that bitraysed be   30
Through false folk; god yeve hem sorwe, amen!
That with hir grete wit and subtiltee
Bitrayse yow! and this commeveth me
To speke, and in effect yow alle I preye,
Beth war of men, and herkeneth what I seye!—

Go, litel book, go litel myn tregedie,
Ther god thy maker yet, er that he dye,
So sende might to make in som comedie!
But litel book, no making thou n'envye,
But subgit be to alle poesye;   40
And kis the steppes, wher-as thou seest pace
Virgile, Ovyde, Omer, Lucan, and Stace.

And for ther is so greet diversitee
In English and in wryting of our tonge,
So preye I god that noon miswryte thee,
Ne thee mismetre for defaute of tonge.
And red wher-so thou be, or elles songe,

That thou be understonde I god beseche!
But yet to purpos of my rather speche.—

The wraththe, as I began yow for to seye,   50
Of Troilus, the Grekes boughten dere;
For thousandes his hondes maden deye,
As he that was with-outen any pere,
Save Ector, in his tyme, as I can here.
But weylaway, save only goddes wille,
Dispitously him slough the fiers Achille.

And whan that he was slayn in this manere,
His lighte goost ful blisfully is went
Up to the holownesse of the seventh spere,
In convers letinge every element;   60
And ther he saugh, with ful avysement,
The erratik sterres, herkeninge armonye
With sownes fulle of hevenish melodye.

And doun from thennes faste he gan avyse
This litel spot of erthe, that with the see
Enbraced is, and fully gan despyse
This wrecched world, and held al vanitee
To respect of the pleyn felicitee
That is in hevene above; and at the laste,
Ther he was slayn, his loking doun he caste;   70

And in him-self he lough right at the wo
Of hem that wepten for his deeth so faste;
And dampned al our werk that folweth so
The blinde lust, the which that may not laste,
And sholden al our herte on hevene caste.
And forth he wente, shortly for to telle,
Ther as Mercurie sorted him to dwelle.—

Swich fyn hath, lo, this Troilus for love,
Swich fyn hath al his grete worthinesse;
Swich fyn hath his estat real above,   80
Swich fyn his lust, swich fyn hath his noblesse;
Swich fyn hath false worldes brotelnesse.
And thus bigan his lovinge of Criseyde,
As I have told, and in this wyse he deyde.

O yonge fresshe folkes, he or she,
In which that love up groweth with your age,
Repeyreth hoom from worldly vanitee,
And of your herte up-casteth the visage
To thilke god that after his image
Yow made, and thinketh al nis but a fayre   90
This world, that passeth sone as floures fayre.

And loveth him, the which that right for love
Upon a cros, our soules for to beye,
First starf, and roos, and sit in hevene a-bove;
For he nil falsen no wight, dar I seye,
That wol his herte al hoolly on him leye.
And sin he best to love is, and most meke,
What nedeth feyned loves for to seke?

Lo here, of Payens corsed olde rytes,
Lo here, what alle hir goddes may availle;   100
Lo here, these wrecched worldes appetytes;
Lo here, the fyn and guerdon for travaille
Of Jove, Appollo, of Mars, of swich rascaille!
Lo here, the forme of olde clerkes speche
In poetrye, if ye hir bokes seche.—

O moral Gower, this book I directe
To thee, and to the philosophical Strode,
To vouchen sauf, ther nede is, to corecte,

Of your benignitees and zeles gode.
And to that sothfast Crist, that starf on rode,   110
With al myn herte of mercy ever I preye;
And to the lord right thus I speke and seye:

Thou oon, and two, and three, eterne on-lyve,
That regnest ay in three and two and oon,
Uncircumscript, and al mayst circumscryve,
Us from visible and invisible foon
Defende; and to thy mercy, everychoon,
So make us, Jesus, for thy grace, digne,
For love of mayde and moder thyn benigne! Amen.

The Legend of Good Women

THE PROLOGE OF .IX. GOODE WIMMEN

A thousand tymes have I herd men telle,
That ther is joye in heven, and peyne in helle;
And I acorde wel that hit is so;
But natheles, yit wot I wel also,
That ther nis noon dwelling in this contree,
That either hath in heven or helle y-be,
Ne may of hit non other weyes witen,
But as he hath herd seyd, or founde hit writen;
For by assay ther may no man hit preve.
But god forbede but men shulde leve   10
Wel more thing then men han seen with yë!
Men shal nat wenen every-thing a lyë
But-if him-self hit seeth, or elles dooth;
For, god wot, thing is never the lasse sooth,
Thogh every wight ne may hit nat y-see.
Bernard the monk ne saugh nat al, parde!
    Than mote we to bokes that we finde,
Through which that olde thinges been in minde,

And to the doctrine of these olde wyse,
Yeve credence, in every skilful wyse,　　20
That tellen of these olde appreved stories,
Of holinesse, of regnes, of victories,
Of love, of hate, of other sundry thinges,
Of whiche I may not maken rehersinges.
And if that olde bokes were a-weye,
Y-loren were of remembrance the keye.
Wel oghte us than honouren and beleve
These bokes, ther we han non other preve.
　　And as for me, thogh that I can but lyte,
On bokes for to rede I me delyte,　　30
And to hem yeve I feyth and ful credence,
And in myn herte have hem in reverence
So hertely, that ther is game noon
That fro my bokes maketh me to goon,
But hit be seldom, on the holyday;
Save, certeynly, whan that the month of May
Is comen, and that I here the foules singe,
And that the floures ginnen for to springe,
Farwel my book and my devocioun!
　　Now have I than swich a condicioun,　　40
That, of alle the floures in the mede,
Than love I most these floures whyte and rede,
Swiche as men callen daysies in our toun.
To hem have I so greet affeccioun,
As I seyde erst, whan comen is the May,
That in my bed ther daweth me no day
That I nam up, and walking in the mede
To seen this flour agein the sonne sprede,
Whan hit upryseth erly by the morwe;
That blisful sighte softneth al my sorwe,　　50
So glad am I whan that I have presence
Of hit, to doon al maner reverence,
As she, that is of alle floures flour,

Fulfilled of al vertu and honour,
And ever y-lyke fair, and fresh of hewe;
And I love hit, and ever y-lyke newe,
And ever shal, til that myn herte dye;
Al swere I nat, of this I wol nat lye,
Ther loved no wight hotter in his lyve.

And whan that hit is eve, I ronne blyve,   60
As sone as ever the sonne ginneth weste,
To seen this flour, how it wol go to reste,
For fere of night, so hateth she derknesse!
Hir chere is pleynly sprad in the brightnesse
Of the sonne, for ther hit wol unclose.
Allas! that I ne had English, ryme or prose,
Suffisant this flour to preyse aright!
But helpeth, ye that han conning and might,
Ye lovers, that can make of sentement;
In this cas oghte ye be diligent   70
To forthren me somwhat in my labour,
Whether ye ben with the leef or with the flour.
For wel I wot, that ye han her-biforn
Of making ropen, and lad awey the corn;
And I come after, glening here and there,
And am ful glad if I may finde an ere
Of any goodly word that ye han left.
And thogh it happen me rehercen eft
That ye han in your fresshe songes sayd,
For-bereth me, and beth nat evel apayd,   80
Sin that ye see I do hit in the honour
Of love, and eek in service of the flour,
Whom that I serve as I have wit or might.
She is the clernesse and the verray light,
That in this derke worlde me wynt and ledeth,
The herte in-with my sorowful brest yow dredeth,
And loveth so sore, that ye ben verrayly
The maistresse of my wit, and nothing I.

My word, my werk, is knit so in your bonde,
That, as an harpe obeyeth to the honde   90
And maketh hit soune after his fingeringe,
Right so mowe ye out of myn herte bringe
Swich vois, right as yow list, to laughe or pleyne.
Be ye my gyde and lady sovereyne;
As to myn erthly god, to yow I calle,
Bothe in this werke and in my sorwes alle.

But wherfor that I spak, to give credence
To olde stories, and doon hem reverence,
And that men mosten more thing beleve
Then men may seen at eye or elles preve?   100
That shal I seyn, whan that I see my tyme;
I may not al at ones speke in ryme.
My besy gost, that thrusteth alwey newe
To seen this flour so yong, so fresh of hewe,
Constreyned me with so gledy desyr,
That in my herte I fele yit the fyr,
That made me to ryse er hit wer day—
And this was now the firste morwe of May—
With dredful herte and glad devocioun,
For to ben at the resureccioun   110
Of this flour, whan that it shuld unclose
Agayn the sonne, that roos as rede as rose,
That in the brest was of the beste that day,
That Agenores doghter ladde away.
And doun on knees anon-right I me sette,
And, as I coude, this fresshe flour I grette;
Kneling alwey, til hit unclosed was,
Upon the smale softe swote gras,
That was with floures swote enbrouded al,
Of swich swetnesse and swich odour over-al,   120
That, for to speke of gomme, or herbe, or tree,
Comparisoun may noon y-maked be;
For hit surmounteth pleynly alle odoures,

And eek of riche beautee alle floures.
Forgeten had the erthe his pore estat
Of winter, that him naked made and mat,
And with his swerd of cold so sore greved;
Now hath the atempre sonne al that releved
That naked was, and clad hit new agayn.
The smale foules, of the seson fayn,   130
That from the panter and the net ben scaped,
Upon the fouler, that hem made a-whaped
In winter, and distroyed had hir brood,
In his despyt, hem thoughte hit did hem good
To singe of him, and in hir song despyse
The foule cherl that, for his covetyse,
Had hem betrayed with his sophistrye.
This was hir song—'the fouler we defye,
And al his craft!' And somme songen clere
Layes of love, that joye hit was to here,   140
In worshipinge and preisinge of hir make.
And, for the newe blisful somers sake,
Upon the braunches ful of blosmes softe,
In hir delyt, they turned hem ful ofte,
And songen, 'blessed be seynt Valentyn!
For on his day I chees yow to be myn,
Withouten repenting, myn herte swete!'
And therwith-al hir bekes gonnen mete,
Yelding honour and humble obeisaunces
To love, and diden hir other observaunces   150
That longeth unto love and to nature;
Construeth that as yow list, I do no cure.
   And tho that hadde doon unkindenesse—
As dooth the tydif, for new-fangelnesse—
Besoghte mercy of hir trespassinge,
And humblely songen hir repentinge,
And sworen on the blosmes to be trewe,
So that hir makes wolde upon hem rewe,

And at the laste maden hir acord.
Al founde they Daunger for a tyme a lord,   160
Yet Pitee, through his stronge gentil might,
Forgaf, and made Mercy passen Right,
Through innocence and ruled curtesye.
But I ne clepe nat innocence folye,
Ne fals pitee, for 'vertu is the mene,'
As Etik saith, in swich manere I mene.
And thus thise foules, voide of al malyce,
Acordeden to love, and laften vyce
Of hate, and songen alle of oon acord,
'Welcome, somer, our governour and lord!'   170
    And Zephirus and Flora gentilly
Yaf to the floures, softe and tenderly,
Hir swote breth, and made hem for to sprede,
As god and goddesse of the floury mede;
In which me thoghte I mighte, day by day,
Dwellen alwey, the joly month of May,
Withouten sleep, withouten mete or drinke.
A-doun ful softely I gan to sinke;
And, leninge on myn elbowe and my syde,
The longe day I shoop me for to abyde   180
For nothing elles, and I shal nat lye,
But for to loke upon the dayesye,
That wel by reson men hit calle may
The 'dayesye' or elles the 'ye of day,'
The emperice and flour of floures alle.
I pray to god that faire mot she falle,
And alle that loven floures, for hir sake!
But natheles, ne wene nat that I make
In preysing of the flour agayn the leef,
No more than of the corn agayn the sheef: 190
For, as to me, nis lever noon ne lother;
I nam with-holden yit with never nother.
Ne I not who serveth leef, ne who the flour;

Wel brouken they hir service or labour;
For this thing is al of another tonne,
Of olde story, er swich thing was begonne.
    Whan that the sonne out of the south gan weste,
And that this flour gan close and goon to reste
For derknesse of the night, the which she dredde,
Hoom to myn hous ful swiftly I me spedde   200
To goon to reste, and erly for to ryse,
To seen this flour to sprede, as I devyse.
And, in a litel herber that I have,
That benched was on turves fresshe y-grave,
I bad men sholde me my couche make;
For deyntee of the newe someres sake,
I bad hem strawen floures on my bed.
Whan I was leyd, and had myn eyen hed,
I fel on slepe in-with an houre or two;
Me mette how I lay in the medew tho,   210
To seen this flour that I so love and drede.
And from a-fer com walking in the mede
The god of love, and in his hande a quene;
And she was clad in real habit grene.
A fret of gold she hadde next hir heer,
And upon that a whyt coroun she beer
With florouns smale, and I shal nat lye;
For al the world, ryght as a dayesye
Y-corouned is with whyte leves lyte,
So were the florouns of hir coroun whyte.   220
For of o perle fyne, oriental,
Hir whyte coroun was y-maked al;
For which the whyte coroun, above the grene,
Made hir lyk a daysie for to sene,
Considered eek hir fret of gold above.
    Y-clothed was this mighty god of love
In silke, enbrouded ful of grene greves,
In-with a fret of rede rose-leves,

The fresshest sin the world was first bigonne.
His gilte heer was corouned with a sonne,   230
In-stede of gold, for hevinesse and wighte;
Therwith me thoughte his face shoon so brighte
That wel unnethes mighte I him beholde;
And in his hande me thoughte I saugh him holde
Two fyry dartes, as the gledes rede;
And aungellyke his winges saugh I sprede.
And al be that men seyn that blind is he,
Al-gate me thoughte that he mighte see;
For sternely on me he gan biholde,
So that his loking doth myn herte colde.   240
And by the hande he held this noble quene,
Corouned with whyte, and clothed al in grene,
So womanly, so benigne, and so meke,
That in this world, thogh that men wolde seke,
Half hir beautee shulde men nat finde
In creature that formed is by kinde.
And therfor may I seyn, as thinketh me,
This song, in preysing of this lady fre.

BALADE

Hyd, Absolon, thy gilte tresses clere;
Ester, ley thou thy meknesse al a-doun;   250
Hyd, Jonathas, al thy frendly manere;
Penalopee, and Marcia Catoun,
Mak of your wyfhod no comparisoun;
Hyde ye your beautes, Isoude and Eleyne,
My lady cometh, that al this may disteyne.

Thy faire body, lat hit nat appere,
Lavyne; and thou, Lucresse of Rome toun,
And Polixene, that boghten love so dere,
And Cleopatre, with al thy passioun,

Hyde ye your trouthe of love and your renoun;   260
And thou, Tisbe, that hast of love swich peyne;
My lady cometh, that al this may disteyne.

Herro, Dido, Laudomia, alle y-fere,
And Phyllis, hanging for thy Demophoun,
And Canace, espyed by thy chere,
Ysiphile, betraysed with Jasoun,
Maketh of your trouthe neyther boost ne soun;
Nor Ypermistre or Adriane, ye tweyne;
My lady cometh, that al this may disteyne.

The Canterbury Tales

THE PROLOGUE

Here biginneth the Book of the Tales of Caunterbury.

Whan that Aprille with his shoures sote
The droghte of Marche hath perced to the rote,
And bathed every veyne in swich licour,
Of which vertu engendred is the flour;
Whan Zephirus eek with his swete breeth
Inspired hath in every holt and heeth
The tendre croppes, and the yonge sonne
Hath in the Ram his halfe cours y-ronne,
And smale fowles maken melodye,
That slepen al the night with open yë,   10
(So priketh hem nature in hir corages):
Than longen folk to goon on pilgrimages
(And palmers for to seken straunge strondes)
To ferne halwes, couthe in sondry londes;
And specially, from every shires ende
Of Engelond, to Caunterbury they wende,
The holy blisful martir for to seke,

That hem hath holpen, whan that they were seke.
   Bifel that, in that seson on a day,
In Southwerk at the Tabard as I lay   20
Redy to wenden on my pilgrimage
To Caunterbury with ful devout corage,
At night was come in-to that hostelrye
Wel nyne and twenty in a companye,
Of sondry folk, by aventure y-falle
In felawshipe, and pilgrims were they alle,
That toward Caunterbury wolden ryde;
The chambres and the stables weren wyde,
And wel we weren esed atte beste.
And shortly, whan the sonne was to reste,   30
So hadde I spoken with hem everichon,
That I was of hir felawshipe anon,
And made forward erly for to ryse,
To take our wey, ther as I yow devyse.
   But natheles, whyl I have tyme and space,
Er that I ferther in this tale pace,
Me thinketh it acordaunt to resoun,
To telle yow al the condicioun
Of ech of hem, so as it semed me,
And whiche they weren, and of what degree;   40
And eek in what array that they were inne:
And at a knight than wol I first biginne.
   A KNIGHT ther was, and that a worthy man,
That fro the tyme that he first bigan
To ryden out, he loved chivalrye,
Trouthe and honour, fredom and curteisye.
Ful worthy was he in his lordes werre,
And therto haddle he riden (no man ferre)
As wel in Cristendom as hethenesse,
And ever honoured for his worthinesse.   50
   At Alisaundre he was, whan it was wonne;
Ful ofte tyme he hadde the bord bigonne

Aboven alle naciouns in Pruce.
In Lettow hadde he reysed and in Ruce,
No Cristen man so ofte of his degree.
In Gernade at the sege eek hadde he be
Of Algezir, and riden in Belmarye.
At Lyeys was he, and at Satalye,
Whan they were wonne; and in the Grete See
At many a noble aryve hadde he be.   60
At mortal batailles hadde he been fiftene,
And foughten for our feith at Tramissene
In listes thryes, and ay slayn his fo.
This ilke worthy knight had been also
Somtyme with the lord of Palatye,
Ageyn another hethen in Turkye:
And evermore he hadde a sovereyn prys.
And though that he were worthy, he was wys,
And of his port as meke as is a mayde.
He never yet no vileinye ne sayde   70
In al his lyf, un-to no maner wight.
He was a verray parfit gentil knight.
But for to tellen yow of his array,
His hors were gode, but he was nat gay.
Of fustian he wered a gipoun
Al bismotered with his habergeoun;
For he was late y-come from his viage,
And wente for to doon his pilgrimage.
    With him ther was his sone, a yong SQUYER,
A lovyere, and a lusty bacheler,   80
With lokkes crulle, as they were leyd in presse.
Of twenty yeer of age he was, I gesse.
Of his stature he was of evene lengthe,
And wonderly deliver, and greet of strengthe.
And he had been somtyme in chivachye,
In Flaundres, in Artoys, and Picardye,
And born him wel, as of so litel space,

H

In hope to stonden in his lady grace.
Embrouded was he, as it were a mede
Al ful of fresshe floures, whyte and rede.   90
Singinge he was, or floytinge, al the day;
He was as fresh as is the month of May.
Short was his goune, with sleves longe and wyde.
Wel coude he sitte on hors, and faire ryde.
He coude songes make and wel endyte,
Juste and eek daunce, and wel purtreye and wryte.
So hote he lovede, that by nightertale
He sleep namore than dooth a nightingale.
Curteys he was, lowly, and servisable,
And carf biforn his fader at the table.   100

A YEMAN hadde he, and servaunts namo
At that tyme, for him liste ryde so;
And he was clad in cote and hood of grene;
A sheef of pecok-arwes brighte and kene
Under his belt he bar ful thriftily;
(Wel coude he dresse his takel yemanly:
His arwes drouped noght with fetheres lowe),
And in his hand he bar a mighty bowe.
A not-heed hadde he, with a broun visage.
Of wode-craft wel coude he al the usage.   110
Upon his arm he bar a gay bracer,
And by his syde a swerd and a bokeler,
And on that other syde a gay daggere,
Harneised wel, and sharp as point of spere;
A Cristofre on his brest of silver shene.
An horn he bar, the bawdrik was of grene;
A forster was he, soothly, as I gesse.

Ther was also a Nonne, a PRIORESSE,
That of hir smyling was ful simple and coy;
Hir gretteste ooth was but by sëynt Loy;   120
And she was cleped madame Eglentyne.
Ful wel she song the service divyne,

Entuned in hir nose ful semely;
And Frensh she spak ful faire and fetisly,
After the scole of Stratford atte Bowe,
For Frensh of Paris was to hir unknowe.
At mete wel y-taught was she with-alle;
She leet no morsel from hir lippes falle,
Ne wette hir fingres in hir sauce depe.
Wel coude she carie a morsel, and wel kepe,   130
That no drope ne fille up-on hir brest.
In curteisye was set ful muche hir lest.
Hir over lippe wyped she so clene,
That in her coppe was no ferthing sene
Of grece, whan she dronken hadde hir draughte.
Ful semely after hir mete she raughte,
And sikerly she was of greet disport,
And ful plesaunt, and amiable of port,
And peyned hir to countrefete chere
Of court, and been estatlich of manere,   140
And to ben holden digne of reverence.
But, for to speken of hir conscience,
She was so charitable and so pitous,
She wolde wepe, if that she sawe a mous
Caught in a trappe, if it were deed or bledde.
Of smale houndes had she, that she fedde
With rosted flesh, or milk and wastel-breed.
But sore weep she if oon of hem were deed,
Or if men smoot it with a yerde smerte:
And al was conscience and tendre herte.   150
Ful semely hir wimpel pinched was;
Hir nose tretys; hir eyen greye as glas;
Hir mouth ful smal, and ther-to softe and reed;
But sikerly she hadde a fair forheed;
It was almost a spanne brood, I trowe;
For, hardily, she was nat undergrowe.
Ful fetis was hir cloke, as I was war.

Of smal coral aboute hir arm she bar
A peire of bedes, gauded al with grene;
And ther-on heng a broche of gold ful shene,   160
On which ther was first write a crowned A,
And after, *Amor vincit omnia.*

Another NONNE with hir hadde she,
That was hir chapeleyne, and PREESTES THREE.

A MONK ther was, a fair for the maistrye,
An out-rydere, that lovede venerye;
A manly man, to been an abbot able.
Ful many a deyntee hors hadde he in stable:
And, whan he rood, men mighte his brydel here
Ginglen in a whistling wind as clere,   170
And eek as loude as dooth the chapel-belle
Ther as this lord was keper of the celle.
The reule of seint Maure or of seint Beneit,
By-cause that it was old and som-del streit,
This ilke monk leet olde thinges pace,
And held after the newe world the space.
He yaf nat of that text a pulled hen,
That seith, that hunters been nat holy men;
Ne that a monk, whan he is cloisterlees,
Is lykned til a fish that is waterlees;   180
This is to seyn, a monk out of his cloistre.
But thilke text held he nat worth an oistre;
And I seyde, his opinioun was good.
What sholde he studie, and make himselven wood,
Upon a book in cloistre alwey to poure,
Or swinken with his handes, and laboure,
As Austin bit? How shal the world be served?
Lat Austin have his swink to him reserved.
Therfore he was a pricasour aright;
Grehoundes he hadde, as swifte as fowel in flight;   190
Of priking and of hunting for the hare
Was al his lust, for no cost wolde he spare.

I seigh his sleves purfiled at the hond
With grys, and that the fyneste of a lond;
And, for to festne his hood under his chin,
He hadde of gold y-wroght a curious pin:
A love-knotte in the gretter ende ther was.
His heed was balled, that shoon as any glas,
And eek his face, as he had been anoint.
He was a lord ful fat and in good point;   200
His eyen stepe, and rollinge in his heed,
That stemed as a forneys of a leed;
His botes souple, his hors in greet estat.
Now certeinly he was a fair prelat;
He was nat pale as a for-pyned goost.
A fat swan loved he best of any roost.
His palfrey was as broun as is a berye.

    A FRERE ther was, a wantown and a merye,
A limitour, a ful solempne man.
In alle the ordres foure is noon that can   210
So muche of daliaunce and fair langage.
He hadde maad ful many a mariage
Of yonge wommen, at his owne cost.
Un-to his ordre he was a noble post.
Ful wel biloved and famulier was he
With frankeleyns over-al in his contree,
And eek with worthy wommen of the toun:
For he had power of confessioun,
As seyde him-self, more than a curat,
For of his ordre he was licentiat.   220
Ful swetely herde he confessioun,
And plesaunt was his absolucioun;
He was an esy man to yeve penaunce
Ther as he wiste to han a good pitaunce;
For unto a povre ordre for to yive
Is signe that a man is wel y-shrive.
For if he yaf, he dorste make avaunt,

He wiste that a man was repentaunt.
For many a man so hard is of his herte,
He may nat wepe al-thogh him sore smerte. 230
Therfore, in stede of weping and preyeres,
Men moot yeve silver to the povre freres.
His tipet was ay farsed ful of knyves
And pinnes, for to yeven faire wyves.
And certeinly he hadde a mery note;
Wel coude he singe and pleyen on a rote.
Of yeddinges he bar utterly the prys.
His nekke whyt was as the flour-de-lys;
Ther-to he strong was as a champioun.
He knew the tavernes wel in every toun, 240
And everich hostiler and tappestere
Bet than a lazar or a beggestere;
For un-to swich a worthy man as he
Acorded nat, as by his facultee,
To have with seke lazars aqueyntaunce.
It is nat honest, it may nat avaunce
For to delen with no swich poraille,
But al with riche and sellers of vitaille.
And over-al, ther as profit sholde aryse,
Curteys he was, and lowly of servyse. 250
Ther nas no man no-wher so vertuous.
He was the beste beggere in his hous;
For thogh a widwe hadde noght a sho,
So plesaunt was his '*In principio*,'
Yet wolde he have a ferthing, er he wente.
His purchas was wel bettre than his rente.
And rage he coude, as it were right a whelpe.
In love-dayes ther coude he muchel helpe.
For there he was nat lyk a cloisterer,
With a thredbar cope, as is a povre scoler, 260
But he was lyk a maister or a pope.
Of double worsted was his semi-cope,

That rounded as a belle out of the presse.
Somwhat he lipsed, for his wantownesse,
To make his English swete up-on his tonge;
And in his harping, whan that he had songe,
His eyen twinkled in his heed aright,
As doon the sterres in the frosty night.
This worthy limitour was cleped Huberd.

A MARCHANT was ther with a forked berd, 270
In mottelee, and hye on horse he sat,
Up-on his heed a Flaundrish bever hat;
His botes clasped faire and fetisly.
His resons he spak ful solempnely,
Souninge alway th'encrees of his winning.
He wolde the see were kept for any thing
Bitwixe Middelburgh and Orewelle.
Wel coude he in eschaunge sheeldes selle.
This worthy man ful wel his wit bisette;
Ther wiste no wight that he was in dette, 280
So estatly was he of his governaunce,
With his bargaynes, and with his chevisaunce.
For sothe he was a worthy man with-alle,
But sooth to seyn, I noot how men him calle.

A CLERK ther was of Oxenford also,
That un-to logik hadde longe y-go.
As lene was his hors as is a rake,
And he nas nat right fat, I undertake;
But loked holwe, and ther-to soberly.
Ful thredbar was his overest courtepy; 290
For he had geten him yet no benefyce,
Ne was so worldly for to have offyce.
For him was lever have at his beddes heed
Twenty bokes, clad in blak or reed,
Of Aristotle and his philosophye,
Than robes riche, or fithele, or gay sautrye.
But al be that he was a philosophre,

Yet hadde he but litel gold in cofre;
But al that he mighte of his freendes hente,
On bokes and on lerninge he it spente,   300
And bisily gan for the soules preye
Of hem that yaf him wher-with to scoleye.
Of studie took he most cure and most hede.
Noght o word spak he more than was nede,
And that was seyd in forme and reverence,
And short and quik, and ful of hy sentence.
Souninge in moral vertu was his speche,
And gladly wolde he lerne, and gladly teche.
    A SERGEANT OF THE LAWE, war and wys,
That often hadde been at the parvys,   310
Ther was also, ful riche of excellence.
Discreet he was, and of greet reverence:
He semed swich, his wordes weren so wyse.
Justyce he was ful often in assyse,
By patente, and by pleyn commissioun;
For his science, and for his heigh renoun
Of fees and robes hadde he many oon.
So greet a purchasour was no-wher noon.
Al was fee simple to him in effect,
His purchasing mighte nat been infect.   320
No-wher so bisy a man as he ther nas,
And yet he semed bisier than he was.
In termes hadde he caas and domes alle,
That from the tyme of king William were falle.
Therto he coude endyte, and make a thing,
Ther coude no wight pinche at his wryting;
And every statut coude he pleyn by rote.
He rood but hoomly in a medlee cote
Girt with a ceint of silk, with barres smale;
Of his array telle I no lenger tale.   330
    A FRANKELEYN was in his companye;
Whyt was his berd, as is the dayesye.

Of his complexioun he was sangwyn.
Wel loved he by the morwe a sop in wyn.
To liven in delyt was ever his wone,
For he was Epicurus owne sone,
That heeld opinioun, that pleyn delyt
Was verraily felicitee parfyt.
An housholdere, and that a greet, was he;
Seint Julian he was in his contree.   340
His breed, his ale, was alwey after oon;
A bettre envyned man was no-wher noon.
With-oute bake mete was never his hous,
Of fish and flesh, and that so plentevous,
It snewed in his hous of mete and drinke,
Of alle deyntees that men coude thinke.
After the sondry sesons of the yeer,
So chaunged he his mete and his soper.
Ful many a fat partrich hadde he in mewe,
And many a breem and many a luce in stewe.   350
Wo was his cook, but-if his sauce were
Poynaunt and sharp, and redy al his gere.
His table dormant in his halle alway
Stood redy covered al the longe day.
At sessiouns ther was he lord and sire;
Ful ofte tyme he was knight of the shire.
An anlas and a gipser al of silk
Heng at his girdel, whyt as morne milk.
A shirreve hadde he been, and a countour;
Was no-wher such a worthy vavasour.   360

   An HABERDASSHER and a CARPENTER,
A WEBBE, a DYERE, and a TAPICER,
Were with us eek, clothed in o liveree,
Of a solempne and greet fraternitee.
Ful fresh and newe hir gere apyked was;
Hir knyves were y-chaped noght with bras,
But al with silver, wroght ful clene and weel,

Hir girdles and hir pouches every-deel.
Wel semed ech of hem a fair burgeys,
To sitten in a yeldhalle on a deys.   370
Everich, for the wisdom that he can,
Was shaply for to been an alderman.
For catel hadde they y-nogh and rente,
And eek hir wyves wolde it wel assente;
And elles certein were they to blame.
It is ful fair to been y-clept '*ma dame*,'
And goon to vigilyës al bifore,
And have a mantel royalliche y-bore.

 A Cook they hadde with hem for the nones,
To boille the chiknes with the marybones,   380
And poudre-marchant tart, and galingale.
Wel coude he knowe a draughte of London ale.
He coude roste, and sethe, and broille, and frye,
Maken mortreux, and wel bake a pye.
But greet harm was it, as it thoughte me,
That on his shine a mormal hadde he;
For blankmanger, that made he with the beste.

 A Shipman was ther, woning fer by weste:
For aught I woot, he was of Dertemouthe.
He rood up-on a rouncy, as he couthe,   390
In a gowne of falding to the knee.
A daggere hanging on a laas hadde he
Aboute his nekke under his arm adoun.
The hote somer had maad his hewe al broun;
And, certeinly, he was a good felawe.
Ful many a draughte of wyn had he y-drawe
From Burdeux-ward, whyl that the chapman sleep.
Of nyce conscience took he no keep.
If that he faught, and hadde the hyer hond,
By water he sente hem hoom to every lond.   400
But of his craft to rekene wel his tydes,
His stremes and his daungers him bisydes,

His herberwe and his mone, his lodemenage,
Ther nas noon swich from Hulle to Cartage.
Hardy he was, and wys to undertake;
With many a tempest hadde his berd been shake.
He knew wel alle the havenes, as they were,
From Gootlond to the cape of Finistere,
And every cryke in Britayne and in Spayne;
His barge y-cleped was the Maudelayne.   410
    With us ther was a DOCTOUR OF PHISYK,
In al this world ne was ther noon him lyk
To speke of phisik and of surgerye;
For he was grounded in astronomye.
He kepte his pacient a ful greet del
In houres, by his magik naturel.
Wel coude he fortunen the ascendent
Of his images for his pacient.
He knew the cause of everich maladye,
Were it of hoot or cold, or moiste, or drye,   420
And where engendred, and of what humour;
He was a verrey parfit practisour.
The cause y-knowe, and of his harm the rote,
Anon he yaf the seke man his bote.
Ful redy hadde he his apothecaries,
To sende him drogges and his letuaries,
For ech of hem made other for to winne;
Hir frendschipe nas nat newe to biginne.
Wel knew he th'olde Esculapius,
And Deiscorides, and eek Rufus,   430
Old Ypocras, Haly, and Galien;
Serapion, Razis, and Avicen;
Averrois, Damascien, and Constantyn;
Bernard, and Gatesden, and Gilbertyn.
Of his diete mesurable was he,
For it was of no superfluitee,
But of greet norissing and digestible.

His studie was but litel on the bible.
In sangwin and in pers he clad was al,
Lyned with taffata and with sendal;   440
And yet he was but esy of dispence;
He kepte that he wan in pestilence.
For gold in phisik is a cordial,
Therfore he lovede gold in special.

    A good WYF was ther of bisyde BATHE,
But she was som-del deef, and that was scathe.
Of clooth-making she hadde swiche an haunt,
She passed hem of Ypres and of Gaunt.
In al the parisshe wyf ne was ther noon
That to th' offring bifore hir sholde goon;   450
And if ther dide, certeyn, so wrooth was she,
That she was out of alle charitee.
Hir coverchiefs ful fyne were of ground;
I dorste swere they weyeden ten pound
That on a Sonday were upon hir heed.
Hir hosen weren of fyn scarlet reed,
Ful streite y-teyd, and shoos ful moiste and newe.
Bold was hir face, and fair, and reed of hewe.
She was a worthy womman al hir lyve,
Housbondes at chirche-dore she hadde fyve,   460
Withouten other companye in youthe;
But therof nedeth nat to speke as nouthe.
And thryes hadde she been at Jerusalem;
She hadde passed many a straunge streem;
At Rome she hadde been, and at Boloigne,
In Galice at seint Jame, and at Coloigne.
She coude muche of wandring by the weye:
Gat-tothed was she, soothly for to seye.
Up-on an amblere esily she sat,
Y-wimpled wel, and on hir heed an hat   470
As brood as is a bokeler or a targe;
A foot-mantel aboute hir hipes large,

And on hir feet a paire of spores sharpe.
In felawschip wel coude she laughe and carpe.
Of remedyes of love she knew perchaunce,
For she coude of that art the olde daunce.

A good man was ther of religioun,
And was a povre PERSOUN of a toun;
But riche he was of holy thoght and werk.
He was also a lerned man, a clerk,   480
That Cristes gospel trewely wolde preche;
His parisshens devoutly wolde he teche.
Benigne he was, and wonder diligent,
And in adversitee ful pacient;
And swich he was y-preved ofte sythes.
Ful looth were him to cursen for his tythes,
But rather wolde he yeven, out of doute,
Un-to his povre parisshens aboute
Of his offring, and eek of his substaunce.
He coude in litel thing han suffisaunce.   490
Wyd was his parisshe, and houses fer a-sonder,
But he ne lafte nat, for reyn ne thonder,
In siknes nor in meschief, to visyte
The ferreste in his parisshe, muche and lyte,
Up-on his feet, and in his hand a staf.
This noble ensample to his sheep he yaf,
That first he wroghte, and afterward he taughte;
Out of the gospel he tho wordes caughte;
And this figure he added eek ther-to,
That if gold ruste, what shal iren do?   500
For if a preest be foul, on whom we truste,
No wonder is a lewed man to ruste;
And shame it is, if a preest take keep,
A shiten shepherde and a clene sheep.
Wel oghte a preest ensample for to yive,
By his clennesse, how that his sheep shold live.
He sette nat his benefice to hyre, .

And leet his sheep encombred in the myre,
And ran to London, un-to sëynt Poules,
To seken him a chaunterie for soules, 510
Or with a bretherhed to been withholde;
But dwelte at hoom, and kepte wel his folde,
So that the wolf ne made it nat miscarie;
He was a shepherde and no mercenarie.
And though he holy were, and vertuous,
He was to sinful man nat despitous,
Ne of his speche daungerous ne digne,
But in his teching discreet and benigne.
To drawen folk to heven by fairnesse
By good ensample, was his bisinesse: 520
But it were any persone obstinat,
What-so he were, of heigh or lowe estat,
Him wolde he snibben sharply for the nones.
A bettre preest, I trowe that nowher noon is.
He wayted after no pompe and reverence,
Ne maked him a spyced conscience,
But Cristes lore, and his apostles twelve,
He taughte, and first he folwed it himselve.

With him ther was a PLOWMAN, was his brother,
That hadde y-lad of dong ful many a fother, 530
A trewe swinker and a good was he,
Livinge in pees and parfit charitee.
God loved he best with al his hole herte
At alle tymes, thogh him gamed or smerte,
And thanne his neighebour right as himselve.
He wolde thresshe, and ther-to dyke and delve,
For Cristes sake, for every povre wight,
Withouten hyre, if it lay in his might.
His tythes payed he ful faire and wel,
Bothe of his propre swink and his catel. 540
In a tabard he rood upon a mere.

Ther was also a Reve and a Millere,

A Somnour and a Pardoner also,
A Maunciple, and my-self; ther were namo.
　　The MILLER was a stout carl, for the nones,
Ful big he was of braun, and eek of bones;
That proved wel, for over-al ther he cam,
At wrastling he wolde have alwey the ram.
He was short-sholdred, brood, a thikke knarre,
Ther nas no dore that he nolde heve of harre,　　550
Or breke it, at a renning, with his heed.
His berd as any sowe or fox was reed,
And ther-to brood, as though it were a spade.
Up-on the cop right of his nose he hade
A werte, and ther-on stood a tuft of heres,
Reed as the bristles of a sowes eres;
His nose-thirles blake were and wyde.
A swerd and bokeler bar he by his syde;
His mouth as greet was as a greet forneys.
He was a janglere and a goliardeys,　　560
And that was most of sinne and harlotryes.
Wel coude he stelen corn, and tollen thryes;
And yet he hadde a thombe of gold, pardee.
A whyt cote and a blew hood wered he.
A baggepype wel coude he blowe and sowne,
And ther-with-al he broghte us out of towne.
　　A gentil MAUNCIPLE was ther of a temple,
Of which achatours mighte take exemple
For to be wyse in bying of vitaille
For whether that he payde, or took by taille,　　570
Algate he wayted so in his achat,
That he was ay biforn and in good stat.
Now is nat that of God a ful fair grace,
That swich a lewed mannes wit shal pace
The wisdom of an heep of lerned men?
Of maistres hadde he mo than thryes ten,
That were of lawe expert and curious;

Of which ther were a doseyn in that hous
Worthy to been stiwardes of rente and lond
Of any lord that is in Engelond,   580
To make him live by his propre good,
In honour dettelees, but he were wood,
Or live as scarsly as him list desire;
And able for to helpen al a shire
In any cas that mighte falle or happe;
And yit this maunciple sette hir aller cappe.

The REVE was a sclendre colerik man,
His berd was shave as ny as ever he can.
His heer was by his eres round y-shorn.
His top was dokked lyk a preest biforn.   590
Ful longe were his legges, and ful lene,
Y-lyk a staf, ther was no calf y-sene.
Wel coude he kepe a gerner and a binne;
Ther was noon auditour coude on him winne.
Wel wiste he, by the droghte, and by the reyn,
The yelding of his seed, and of his greyn.
His lordes sheep, his neet, his dayerye,
His swyn, his hors, his stoor, and his pultrye,
Was hoolly in this reves governing,
And by his covenaunt yaf the rekening,   600
Sin that his lord was twenty yeer of age;
Ther coude no man bringe him in arrerage.
Ther nas baillif, ne herde, ne other hyne,
That he ne knew his sleighte and his covyne;
They were adrad of him, as of the deeth.
His woning was ful fair up-on an heeth,
With grene treës shadwed was his place.
He coude bettre than his lord purchace.
Ful riche he was astored prively,
His lord wel coude he plesen subtilly,   610
To yeve and lene him of his owne good,
And have a thank, and yet a cote and hood.

In youthe he lerned hadde a good mister;
He was a wel good wrighte, a carpenter.
This reve sat up-on a ful good stot,
That was al pomely grey, and highte Scot.
A long surcote of pers up-on he hade,
And by his syde he bar a rusty blade.
Of Northfolk was this reve, of which I telle,
Bisyde a toun men clepen Baldeswelle. 620
Tukked he was, as is a frere, aboute,
And ever he rood the hindreste of our route.

 A SOMNOUR was ther with us in that place,
That hadde a fyr-reed cherubinnes face,
For sawcefleem he was, with eyen narwe.
As hoot he was, and lecherous, as a sparwe;
With scalled browes blake, and piled berd;
Of his visage children were aferd.
Ther nas quik-silver, litarge, ne brimstoon,
Boras, ceruce, ne oille of tartre noon, 630
Ne oynement that wolde clense and byte,
That him mighte helpen of his whelkes whyte,
Nor of the knobbes sittinge on his chekes.
Wel loved he garleek, oynons, and eek lekes,
And for to drinken strong wyn, reed as blood.
Than wolde he speke, and crye as he were wood.
And whan that he wel dronken hadde the wyn,
Than wolde he speke no word but Latyn.
A fewe termes hadde he, two or three,
That he had lerned out of som decree; 640
No wonder is, he herde it al the day;
And eek ye knowen wel, how that a jay
Can clepen 'Watte,' as well as can the pope.
But who-so coude in other thing him grope,
Thanne hadde he spent al his philosophye;
Ay '*Questio quid iuris*' wolde he crye.
He was a gentil harlot and a kinde;

I

A bettre felawe sholde men noght finde.
He wolde suffre, for a quart of wyn,
A good felawe to have his concubyn   650
A twelf-month, and excuse him atte fulle:
Ful prively a finch eek coude he pulle.
And if he fond o-wher a good felawe,
He wolde techen him to have non awe,
In swich cas, of the erchedeknes curs,
But-if a mannes soule were in his purs;
For in his purs he sholde y-punisshed be.
'Purs is the erchedeknes helle,' seyde he.
But wel I woot he lyed right in dede;
Of cursing oghte ech gilty man him drede—   660
For curs wol slee, right as assoilling saveth—
And also war him of a *significavit*.
In daunger hadde he at his owne gyse
The yonge girles of the diocyse,
And knew hir counseil, and was al hir reed.
A gerland hadde he set up-on his heed,
As greet as it were for an ale-stake;
A bokeler hadde he maad him of a cake.

With him ther rood a gentil PARDONER
Of Rouncival, his freend and his compeer,   670
That streight was comen fro the court of Rome.
Ful loude he song, 'Com hider, love, to me.'
This somnour bar to him a stif burdoun,
Was never trompe of half so greet a soun.
This pardoner hadde heer as yelow as wex,
But smothe it heng, as dooth a strike of flex;
By ounces henge his lokkes that he hadde,
And ther-with he his shuldres over-spradde;
But thinne it lay, by colpons oon and oon;
But hood, for jolitee, ne wered he noon,   680
For it was trussed up in his walet.
Him thoughte, he rood al of the newe jet;

Dischevele, save his cappe, he rood al bare.
Swiche glaringe eyen hadde he as an hare.
A vernicle hadde he sowed on his cappe.
His walet lay biforn him in his lappe,
Bret-ful of pardoun come from Rome al hoot.
A voys he hadde as smal as hath a goot.
No berd hadde he, he never sholde have,
As smothe it was as it were late y-shave;   690
I trowe he were a gelding or a mare.
But of his craft, fro Berwik into Ware,
Ne was ther swich another pardoner.
For in his male he hadde a pilwe-beer,
Which that, he seyde, was our lady veyl:
He seyde, he hadde a gobet of the seyl
That sëynt Peter hadde, whan that he wente
Up-on the see, til Jesu Crist him hente.
He hadde a croys of latoun, ful of stones,
And in a glas he hadde pigges bones.   700
But with thise relikes, whan that he fond
A povre person dwelling up-on lond,
Up-on a day he gat him more moneye
Than that the person gat in monthes tweye.
And thus, with feyned flaterye and japes,
He made the person and the peple his apes.
But trewely to tellen, atte laste,
He was in chirche a noble ecclesiaste.
Wel coude he rede a lessoun or a storie,
But alderbest he song an offertorie;   710
For wel he wiste, whan that song was songe,
He moste preche, and wel affyle his tonge,
To winne silver, as he ful wel coude;
Therefore he song so meriely and loude.
    Now have I told you shortly, in a clause,
Th'estat, th'array, the nombre, and eek the cause
Why that assembled was this companye

In Southwerk, at this gentil hostelrye,
That highte the Tabard, faste by the Belle.
But now is tyme to yow for to telle   720
How that we baren us that ilke night,
Whan we were in that hostelrye alight.
And after wol I telle of our viage,
And al the remenaunt of our pilgrimage.
But first I pray yow, of your curteisye,
That ye n'arette it nat my vileinye,
Thogh that I pleynly speke in this matere,
To telle yow hir wordes and hir chere;
Ne thogh I speke hir wordes properly.
For this ye knowen al-so wel as I,   730
Who-so shal telle a tale after a man,
He moot reherce, as ny as ever he can,
Everich a word, if it be in his charge,
Al speke he never so rudeliche and large;
Or elles he moot telle his tale untrewe,
Or feyne thing, or finde wordes newe.
He may nat spare, al-thogh he were his brother;
He moot as wel seye o word as another.
Crist spak him-self ful brode in holy writ,
And wel ye woot, no vileinye is it.   740
Eek Plato seith, who-so that can him rede,
The wordes mote be cosin to the dede.
Also I prey yow to foryeve it me,
Al have I nat set folk in hir degree
Here in this tale, as that they sholde stonde;
My wit is short, ye may wel understonde.

     Greet chere made our hoste us everichon,
And to the soper sette us anon;
And served us with vitaille at the beste.
Strong was the wyn, and wel to drinke us leste.   750
A semely man our hoste was with-alle
For to han been a marshal in an halle;

A large man he was with eyen stepe,
A fairer burgeys is ther noon in Chepe:
Bold of his speche, and wys, and wel y-taught,
And of manhod him lakkede right naught.
Eek therto he was right a mery man,
And after soper pleyen he bigan,
And spak of mirthe amonges othere thinges,
Whan that we hadde maad our rekeninges;   760
And seyde thus: 'Now, lordinges, trewely,
Ye been to me right welcome hertely:
For by my trouthe, if that I shal nat lye,
I ne saugh this yeer so mery a companye
At ones in this herberwe as is now.
Fayn wolde I doon yow mirthe, wiste I how.
And of a mirthe I am right now bithoght,
To doon yow ese, and it shal coste noght.

   Ye goon to Caunterbury; God yow spede,
The blisful martir quyte yow your mede.   770
And wel I woot, as ye goon by the weye,
Ye shapen yow to talen and to pleye;
For trewely, confort ne mirthe is noon
To ryde by the weye doumb as a stoon;
And therfore wol I maken yow disport,
As I seyde erst, and doon yow som confort.
And if yow lyketh alle, by oon assent,
Now for to stonden at my jugement,
And for to werken as I shal yow seye,
To-morwe, whan ye ryden by the weye,   780
Now, by my fader soule, that is deed,
But ye be merye, I wol yeve yow myn heed.
Hold up your hond, withouten more speche.'

   Our counseil was nat longe for to seche;
Us thoughte it was noght worth to make it wys,
And graunted him withouten more avys,
And bad him seye his verdit, as him leste.

'Lordinges,' quod he, 'now herkneth for the
    beste;
But tak it not, I prey yow, in desdeyn;
This is the poynt, to speken short and pleyn,   790
That ech of yow, to shorte with your weye,
In this viage, shal telle tales tweye,
To Caunterbury-ward, I mene it so,
And hom-ward he shal tellen othere two,
Of aventures that whylom han bifalle.
And which of yow that bereth him best of alle,
That is to seyn, that telleth in this cas
Tales of best sentence and most solas,
Shal have a soper at our aller cost
Here in this place, sitting by this post,   800
Whan that we come agayn fro Caunterbury.
And for to make yow the more mery,
I wol my-selven gladly with yow ryde,
Right at myn owne cost, and be your gyde.
And who-so wol my jugement withseye
Shal paye al that we spenden by the weye.
And if ye vouche-sauf that it be so,
Tel me anon, with-outen wordes mo,
And I wol erly shape me therfore.'

This thing was graunted, and our othes swore 810
With ful glad herte, and preyden him also
That he wold vouche-sauf for to do so,
And that he wolde been our governour,
And of our tales juge and reportour,
And sette a soper at a certeyn prys;
And we wold reuled been at his devys,
In heigh and lowe; and thus, by oon assent,
We been acorded to his jugement.
And ther-up-on the wyn was fet anon;
We dronken, and to reste wente echon,   820
With-outen any lenger taryinge.

A-morwe, whan that day bigan to springe,
Up roos our host, and was our aller cok,
And gadrede us togidre, alle in a flok,
And forth we riden, a litel more than pas,
Un-to the watering of seint Thomas.
And there our host bigan his hors areste,
And seyde; 'Lordinges, herkneth, if yow leste.
Ye woot your forward, and I it yow recorde.
If even-song and morwe-song acorde,   830
Lat see now who shal telle the firste tale.
As ever mote I drinke wyn or ale,
Who-so be rebel to my jugement
Shal paye for al that by the weye is spent.
Now draweth cut, er that we ferrer twinne;
He which that hath the shortest shal biginne.
Sire knight,' quod he, 'my maister and my lord,
Now draweth cut, for that is myn acord.
Cometh neer,' quod he, 'my lady prioresse;
And ye, sir clerk, lat be your shamfastnesse,   840
Ne studieth noght; ley hond to, every man.'
   Anon to drawen every wight bigan,
And shortly for to tellen, as it was,
Were it by aventure, or sort, or cas,
The sothe is this, the cut fil to the knight,
Of which ful blythe and glad was every wight;
And telle he moste his tale, as was resoun,
By forward and by composicioun,
As ye han herd; what nedeth wordes mo?
And whan this gode man saugh it was so,   850
As he that wys was and obedient
To kepe his forward by his free assent,
He seyde: 'Sin I shal beginne the game,
What, welcome be the cut, a Goddes name!
Now lat us ryde, and herkneth what I seye.'
   And with that word we riden forth our weye;

And he bigan with right a mery chere
His tale anon, and seyde in this manere.

THE PARDONER'S TALE

In Flaundres whylom was a companye
Of yonge folk, that haunteden folye,
As ryot, hasard, stewes, and tavernes,
Wher-as, with harpes, lutes, and giternes,
They daunce and pleye at dees bothe day and night,
And ete also and drinken over hir might,
Thurgh which they doon the devel sacrifyse
With-in that develes temple, in cursed wyse,
By superfluitee abhominable;
Hir othes been so grete and so dampnable,   10
That it is grisly for to here hem swere;
Our blissed lordes body they to-tere;
Hem thoughte Jewes rente him noght y-nough;
And ech of hem at otheres sinne lough.
And right anon than comen tombesteres
Fetys and smale, and yonge fruytesteres,
Singers with harpes, baudes, wafereres,
Whiche been the verray develes officeres
To kindle and blowe the fyr of lecherye,
That is annexed un-to glotonye;   20
The holy writ take I to my witnesse,
That luxurie is in wyn and dronkenesse.

Lo, how that dronken Loth, unkindely,
Lay by his doghtres two, unwitingly;
So dronke he was, he niste what he wroghte.

Herodes, (who-so wel the stories soghte),
Whan he of wyn was replet at his feste,
Right at his owene table he yaf his heste
To sleen the Baptist John ful giltelees.

Senek seith eek a good word doutelees;   30
He seith, he can no difference finde

Bitwix a man that is out of his minde
And a man which that is dronkelewe,
But that woodnesse, y-fallen in a shrewe,
Persevereth lenger than doth dronkenesse.
O glotonye, ful of cursednesse,
O cause first of our confusioun,
O original of our dampnacioun,
Til Crist had boght us with his blood agayn!
Lo, how dere, shortly for to sayn,   40
Aboght was thilke cursed vileinye;
Corrupt was al this world for glotonye!
    Adam our fader, and his wyf also,
Fro Paradys to labour and to wo
Were driven for that vyce, it is no drede;
For whyl that Adam fasted, as I rede,
He was in Paradys; and whan that he
Eet of the fruyt defended on the tree,
Anon he was out-cast to wo and peyne.
O glotonye, on thee wel oghte us pleyne!   50
O, wiste a man how many maladyes
Folwen of excesse and of glotonyes,
He wolde been the more mesurable
Of his diete, sittinge at his table.
Allas! the shorte throte, the tendre mouth,
Maketh that, Est and West, and North and South,
In erthe, in eir, in water men to-swinke
To gete a glotoun deyntee mete and drinke!
Of this matere, o Paul, wel canstow trete,
'Mete un-to wombe, and wombe eek un-to mete,   60
Shal god destroyen bothe,' as Paulus seith.
Allas! a foul thing is it, by my feith,
To seye this word, and fouler is the dede,
Whan man so drinketh of the whyte and rede,
That of his throte he maketh his privee,
Thurgh thilke cursed superfluitee.

The apostel weping seith ful pitously,
'Ther walken many of whiche yow told have I,
I seye it now weping with pitous voys,
That they been enemys of Cristes croys,   70
Of whiche the ende is deeth, wombe is her god.'
O wombe! O bely! O stinking cod,
Fulfild of donge and of corrupcioun!
At either ende of thee foul is the soun.
How greet labour and cost is thee to finde!
Thise cokes, how they stampe, and streyne, and grinde,
And turnen substaunce in-to accident,
To fulfille al thy likerous talent!
Out of the harde bones knokke they
The mary, for they caste noght a-wey   80
That may go thurgh the golet softe and swote;
Of spicerye, of leef, and bark, and rote
Shal been his sauce y-maked by delyt,
To make him yet a newer appetyt.
But certes, he that haunteth swich delyces
Is deed, whyl that he liveth in tho vyces.

    A lecherous thing is wyn, and dronkenesse
Is ful of stryving and of wrecchednesse.
O dronke man, disfigured is thy face,
Sour is thy breeth, foul artow to embrace,   90
And thurgh thy dronke nose semeth the soun
As though thou seydest ay 'Sampsoun, Sampsoun';
And yet, god wot, Sampsoun drank never no wyn.
Thou fallest, as it were a stiked swyn;
Thy tonge is lost, and al thyn honest cure;
For dronkenesse is verray sepulture
Of mannes wit and his discrecioun.
In whom that drinke hath dominacioun,
He can no conseil kepe, it is no drede.
Now kepe yow fro the whyte and fro the rede,   100
And namely fro the whyte wyn of Lepe,

That is to selle in Fish-strete or in Chepe.
This wyn of Spayne crepeth subtilly
In othere wynes, growing faste by,
Of which ther ryseth swich fumositee,
That whan a man hath dronken draughtes three,
And weneth that he be at hoom in Chepe,
He is in Spayne, right at the toune of Lepe,
Nat at the Rochel, ne at Burdeux toun;
And thanne wol he seye, 'Sampsoun, Sampsoun.'   110
   But herkneth, lordings, o word, I yow preye,
That alle the sovereyn actes, dar I seye,
Of victories in th'olde testament,
Thurgh verray god, that is omnipotent,
Were doon in abstinence and in preyere;
Loketh the Bible, and ther ye may it lere.
   Loke, Attila, the grete conquerour,
Deyde in his sleep, with shame and dishonour,
Bledinge ay at his nose in dronkenesse;
A capitayn shoulde live in sobrenesse.   120
And over al this, avyseth yow right wel
What was comaunded un-to Lamuel—
Nat Samuel, but Lamuel, seye I—
Redeth the Bible, and finde it expresly
Of wyn-yeving to hem that han justyse.
Na-more of this, for it may wel suffyse.
   And now that I have spoke of glotonye,
Now wol I yow defenden hasardrye.
Hasard is verray moder of lesinges,
And of deceite, and cursed forsweringes,   130
Blaspheme of Crist, manslaughtre, and wast also
Of catel and of tyme; and forthermo,
It is repreve and contrarie of honour
For to ben holde a commune hasardour.
And ever the hyër he is of estaat,
The more is he holden desolaat.

If that a prince useth hasardrye,
In alle governaunce and policye
He is, as by commune opinioun,
Y-holde the lasse in reputacioun.   140
   Stilbon, that was a wys embassadour,
Was sent to Corinthe, in ful greet honour,
Fro Lacidomie, to make hir alliaunce.
And whan he cam, him happede, par chaunce,
That alle the grettest that were of that lond,
Pleyinge atte hasard he hem fond.
For which, as sone as it mighte be,
He stal him hoom agayn to his contree,
And seyde, 'ther wol I nat lese my name;
N' I wol nat take on me so greet defame,   150
Yow for to allye un-to none hasardours.
Sendeth othere wyse embassadours;
For, by my trouthe, me were lever dye,
Than I yow sholde to hasardours allye.
For ye that been so glorious in honours
Shul nat allyen yow with hasardours
As by my wil, ne as by my tretee.'
This wyse philosophre thus seyde he.
   Loke eek that, to the king Demetrius
The king of Parthes, as the book seith us,   160
Sente him a paire of dees of gold in scorn,
For he hadde used hasard ther-biforn;
For which he heeld his glorie or his renoun
At no value or reputacioun.
Lordes may finden other maner pley
Honeste y-nough to dryve the day awey.
   Now wol I speke of othes false and grete
A word or two, as olde bokes trete.
Gret swering is a thing abhominable,
And false swering is yet more reprevable.   170
The heighe god forbad swering at al,

Witnesse on Mathew; but in special
Of swering seith the holy Jeremye,
'Thou shalt seye sooth thyn othes, and nat lye,
And swere in dome, and eek in rightwisnesse;'
But ydel swering is a cursednesse.
Bihold and see, that in the firste table
Of heighe goddes hestes honurable,
How that the seconde heste of him is this—
'Tak nat my name in ydel or amis.'   180
Lo, rather he forbedeth swich swering
Than homicyde or many a cursed thing;
I seye that, as by ordre, thus it stondeth;
This knowen, that his hestes understondeth,
How that the second heste of god is that.
And forther over, I wol thee telle al plat,
That vengeance shal nat parten from his hous,
That of his othes is to outrageous.
'By goddes precious herte, and by his nayles,
And by the blode of Crist, that it is in Hayles,   190
Seven is my chaunce, and thyn is cink and treye;
By goddes armes, if thou falsly pleye,
This dagger shal thurgh-out thyn herte go'—
This fruyt cometh of the bicched bones two,
Forswering, ire, falsnesse, homicyde.
Now, for the love of Crist that for us dyde,
Leveth your othes, bothe grete and smale;
But, sirs, now wol I telle forth my tale.

Thise ryotoures three, of whiche I telle,
Longe erst er pryme rong of any belle,   200
Were set hem in a taverne for to drinke;
And as they satte, they herde a belle clinke
Biforn a cors, was caried to his grave;
That oon of hem gan callen to his knave,
'Go bet,' quod he, 'and axe redily,

What cors is this that passeth heer forby;
And look that thou reporte his name wel.'
  'Sir,' quod this boy, 'it nedeth never-a-del.
It was me told, er ye cam heer, two houres;
He was, pardee, an old felawe of youres;   210
And sodeynly he was y-slayn to-night,
For-dronke, as he sat on his bench upright;
Ther cam a privee theef, men clepeth Deeth,
That in this contree al the peple sleeth,
And with his spere he smoot his herte a-two,
And wente his wey with-outen wordes mo.
He hath a thousand slayn this pestilence:
And, maister, er ye come in his presence,
Me thinketh that it were necessarie
For to be war of swich an adversarie: 220
Beth redy for to mete him evermore.
Thus taughte me my dame, I sey na-more.'
  'By seinte Marie,' seyde this taverner,
'The child seith sooth, for he hath slayn this yeer,
Henne over a myle, with-in a greet village,
Both man and womman, child and hyne, and page.
I trowe his habitacioun be there;
To been avysed greet wisdom it were,
Er that he dide a man a dishonour.'
  'Ye, goddes armes,' quod this ryotour,   230
'Is it swich peril with him for to mete?
I shal him seke by wey and eek by strete,
I make avow to goddes digne bones!
Herkneth, felawes, we three been al ones;
Lat ech of us holde up his hond til other,
And ech of us bicomen otheres brother,
And we wol sleen this false traytour Deeth;
He shal be slayn, which that so many sleeth,
By goddes dignitee, er it be night.'
  Togidres han thise three her trouthes plight,   240

To live and dyen ech of hem for other,
As though he were his owene y-boren brother.
And up they sterte al dronken, in this rage,
And forth they goon towardes that village,
Of which the taverner had spoke biforn,
And many a grisly ooth than han they sworn,
And Cristes blessed body they to-rente—
'Deeth shal be deed, if that they may him hente.'

Whan they han goon nat fully half a myle,
Right as they wolde han troden over a style,   250
An old man and a povre with hem mette.
This olde man ful mekely hem grette,
And seyde thus, 'now, lordes, god yow see!'

The proudest of thise ryotoures three
Answerde agayn, 'what? carl, with sory grace,
Why artow al forwrapped save thy face?
Why livestow so longe in so greet age?'

This olde man gan loke in his visage,
And seyde thus, 'for I ne can nat finde
A man, though that I walked in-to Inde,   260
Neither in citee nor in no village,
That wolde chaunge his youthe for myn age;
And therfore moot I han myn age stille,
As longe time as it is goddes wille.

Ne deeth, allas! ne wol nat han my lyf;
Thus walke I, lyk a restelees caityf,
And on the ground, which is my modres gate,
I knokke with my staf, bothe erly and late,
And seye, "leve moder, leet me in!
Lo, how I vanish, flesh, and blood, and skin!   270
Allas! whan shul my bones been at reste?
Moder, with yow wolde I chaunge my cheste,
That in my chambre longe tyme hath be,
Ye! for an heyre clout to wrappe me!"
But yet to me she wol nat do that grace,

For which ful pale and welked is my face.
　　But, sirs, to yow it is no curteisye
To speken to an old man vileinye,
But he trespasse in worde, or elles in dede.
In holy writ ye may your-self wel rede, 280
"Agayns an old man, hoor upon his heed,
Ye sholde aryse;" wherfor I yeve yow reed,
Ne dooth un-to an old man noon harm now,
Na-more than ye wolde men dide to yow
In age, if that ye so longe abyde;
And god be with yow, wher ye go or ryde.
I moot go thider as I have to go.'
　　'Nay, olde cherl, by god, thou shalt nat so,'
Seyde this other hasardour anon;
'Thou partest nat so lightly, by seint John! 290
Thou spak right now of thilke traitour Deeth,
That in this contree alle our frendes sleeth.
Have heer my trouthe, as thou art his aspye,
Tel wher he is, or thou shalt it abye,
By god, and by the holy sacrament!
For soothly thou art oon of his assent,
To sleen us yonge folk, thou false theef!'
　　'Now, sirs,' quod he, 'if that yow be so leef
To finde Deeth, turne up this croked wey,
For in that grove I lafte him, by my fey, 300
Under a tree, and ther he wol abyde;
Nat for your boost he wol him no-thing hyde.
See ye that ook? right ther ye shul him finde.
God save yow, that boghte agayn mankinde,
And yow amende!'—thus seyde this olde man.
And everich of thise ryotoures ran,
Til he cam to that tree, and ther they founde
Of florins fyne of golde y-coyned rounde
Wel ny an eighte busshels, as hem thoughte.
No lenger thanne after Deeth they soughte, 310

But ech of hem so glad was of that sighte,
For that the florins been so faire and brighte,
That doun they sette hem by this precious hord.
The worste of hem he spake the firste word.
   'Brethren,' quod he, 'tak kepe what I seye;
My wit is greet, though that I bourde and pleye.
This tresor hath fortune un-to us yiven,
In mirthe and jolitee our lyf to liven,
And lightly as it comth, so wol we spende.
Ey! goddes precious dignitee! who wende   320
To-day, that we sholde han so fair a grace?
But mighte this gold be caried fro this place
Hoom to myn hous, or elles un-to youres—
For wel ye woot that al this gold is oures—
Than were we in heigh felicitee.
But trewely, by daye it may nat be;
Men wolde seyn that we were theves stronge,
And for our owene tresor doon us honge.
This tresor moste y-caried be by nighte
As wysly and as slyly as it mighte.   330
Wherfore I rede that cut among us alle
Be drawe, and lat see wher the cut wol falle;
And he that hath the cut with herte blythe
Shal renne to the toune, and that ful swythe,
And bringe us breed and wyn ful prively.
And two of us shul kepen subtilly
This tresor wel; and, if he wol nat tarie,
Whan it is night, we wol this tresor carie
By oon assent, wher-as us thinketh best.'
That oon of hem the cut broughte in his fest,   340
And bad hem drawe, and loke wher it wol falle;
And it fil on the yongeste of hem alle;
And forth toward the toun he wente anon.
And al-so sone as that he was gon,
That oon of hem spak thus un-to that other,

K

'Thou knowest wel thou art my sworne brother,
Thy profit wol I telle thee anon.
Thou woost wel that our felawe is agon;
And heer is gold, and that ful greet plentee,
That shal departed been among us three.   350
But natheles, if I can shape it so
That it departed were among us two
Hadde I nat doon a freendes torn to thee?'
     That other answerde, 'I noot how that may be;
He woot how that the gold is with us tweye,
What shal we doon, what shal we to him seye?'
     'Shal it be conseil?' seyde the firste shrewe,
'And I shal tellen thee, in wordes fewe,
What we shal doon, and bringe it wel aboute.
     'I graunte,' quod that other, 'out of doute,   360
That, by my trouthe, I wol thee nat biwreye."
     'Now,' quod the firste, 'thou woost wel we be tweye,
And two of us shul strenger be than oon.
Look whan that he is set, and right anoon
Arys, as though thou woldest with him pleye;
And I shal ryve him thurgh the sydes tweye
Whyl that thou strogelest with him as in game,
And with thy dagger look thou do the same;
And than shal al this gold departed be,
My dere freend, bitwixen me and thee;   370
Than may we bothe our lustes al fulfille,
And pleye at dees right at our owene wille.'
And thus acorded been thise shrewes tweye
To sleen the thridde, as ye han herd me seye.
     This yongest, which that wente un-to the toun,
Ful ofte in herte he rolleth up and doun
The beautee of thise florins newe and brighte.
'O lord!' quod he, 'if so were that I mighte
Have al this tresor to my-self allone,
Ther is no man that liveth under the trone   380

Of god, that sholde live so mery as I!'
And atte laste the feend, our enemy,
Putte in his thought that he shold poyson beye,
With which he mighte sleen his felawes tweye;
For-why the feend fond him in swich lyvinge,
That he had leve him to sorwe bringe,
For this was outrely his fulle entente
To sleen hem bothe, and never to repente.
And forth he gooth, no lenger wolde he tarie,
Into the toun, un-to a pothecarie,   390
And preyed him, that he him wolde selle
Som poyson, that he mighte his rattes quelle;
And eek ther was a polcat in his hawe,
That, as he seyde, his capouns hadde y-slawe,
And fayn he wolde wreke him, if he mighte,
On vermin, that destroyed him by nighte.

 The pothecarie answerde, 'and thou shalt have
A thing that, al-so god my soule save,
In al this world ther nis no creature,
That ete or dronke hath of this confiture   400
Noght but the mountance of a corn of whete,
That he ne shal his lyf anon forlete;
Ye, sterve he shal, and that in lasse whyle
Than thou wolt goon a paas nat but a myle;
This poyson is so strong and violent.'

 This cursed man hath in his hond y-hent
This poyson in a box, and sith he ran
In-to the nexte strete, un-to a man,
And borwed of him large botels three;
And in the two his poyson poured he;   410
The thridde he kepte clene for his drinke.
For al the night he shoop him for to swinke
In caryinge of the gold out of that place.
And whan this ryotour, with sory grace,
Had filled with wyn his grete botels three,

To his felawes agayn repaireth he.

What nedeth it to sermone of it more?
For right as they had cast his deeth bifore,
Right so they han him slayn, and that anon.
And whan that this was doon, thus spak that oon,   420
'Now lat us sitte and drinke, and make us merie,
And afterward we wol his body berie.'
And with that word it happed him, par cas,
To take the botel ther the poyson was,
And drank, and yaf his felawe drinke also,
For which anon they storven bothe two.

But, certes, I suppose that Avicen
Wroot never in no canon, ne in no fen,
Mo wonder signes of empoisoning
Than hadde thise wrecches two, er hir ending.   430
Thus ended been thise homicydes two,
And eek the false empoysoner also.

O cursed sinne, ful of cursednesse!
O traytours homicyde, o wikkednesse!
O glotonye, luxurie, and hasardrye!
Thou blasphemour of Crist with vileinye
And othes grete, of usage and of pryde!
Allas! mankinde, how may it bityde,
That to thy creatour which that thee wroghte,
And with his precious herte-blood thee boghte,   440
Thou art so fals and so unkinde, allas!

Now, goode men, god forgeve yow your trespas,
And ware yow fro the sinne of avaryce.
Myn holy pardoun may yow alle waryce,
So that ye offre nobles or sterlinges,
Or elles silver broches, spones, ringes.
Boweth your heed under this holy bulle!
Cometh up, ye wyves, offreth of your wolle!
Your name I entre heer in my rolle anon;

In-to the blisse of hevene shul ye gon;   450
I yow assoile, by myn heigh power,
Yow that wol offre, as clene and eek as cleer
As ye were born; and, lo, sirs, thus I preche.
And Jesu Crist, that is our soules leche,
So graunte yow his pardon to receyve;
For that is best; I wol yow nat deceyve.

But sirs, o word forgat I in my tale,
I have relikes and pardon in my male,
As faire as any man in Engelond,
Whiche were me yeven by the popes hond.   460
If any of yow wol, of devocioun,
Offren, and han myn absolucioun,
Cometh forth anon, and kneleth heer adoun,
And mekely receyveth my pardoun:
Or elles, taketh pardon as ye wende,
Al newe and fresh, at every tounes ende,
So that ye offren alwey newe and newe
Nobles and pens, which that be gode and trewe.
It is an honour to everich that is heer,   470
That ye mowe have a suffisant pardoneer
T'assoille yow, in contree as ye ryde,
For aventures which that may bityde.
Peraventure ther may falle oon or two
Doun of his hors, and breke his nekke atwo.
Look which a seuretee is it to yow alle
That I am in your felaweship y-falle,
That may assoille yow, bothe more and lasse,
Whan that the soule shal fro the body passe.
I rede that our hoste heer shal biginne,
For he is most envoluped in sinne.   480
Com forth, sir hoste, and offre first anon,
And thou shalt kisse the reliks everichon,
Ye, for a grote! unbokel anon thy purs.'
    'Nay, nay,' quod he, 'than have I Cristes curs!

Lat be,' quod he, 'it shal nat be, so thee'ch!
Thou woldest make me kisse thyn old breech,
And swere it were a relik of a seint, . . .

   This pardoner answerde nat a word;
So wrooth he was, no word ne wolde he seye.

   'Now,' quod our host, 'I wol no lenger pleye   490
With thee, ne with noon other angry man.'
But right anon the worthy Knight bigan,
Whan that he saugh that al the peple lough,
'Na-more of this, for it is right y-nough;
Sir Pardoner, be glad and mery of chere;
And ye, sir host, that been to me so dere,
I prey yow that ye kisse the Pardoner.
And Pardoner, I prey thee, drawe thee neer,
And, as we diden, lat us laughe and pleye.'
Anon they kiste, and riden forth hir weye.   500

FROM CHAUCER'S PROSE

The Parson's Tale

SEQUITUR DE ACCIDIA

After the sinnes of Envie and of Ire, now wol I speken of
the sinne of Accidie. For Envye blindeth the herte of a man,
and Ire troubleth a man; and Accidie maketh him hevy,
thoghtful, and wrawe./ Envye and Ire maken bitternesse
in herte; which bitternesse is moder of Accidie, and
binimeth him the love of alle goodnesse. Thanne is
Accidie the anguissh of a trouble herte; and seint Augustin
seith: 'it is anoy of goodnesse and joye of harm.'/ Certes,
this is a dampnable sinne; for it doth wrong to Jesu
Crist, in-as-muche as it binimeth the service that men   10
oghte doon to Crist with alle diligence, as seith Salomon./
But Accidie dooth no swich diligence; he dooth alle thing

with anoy, and with wrawnesse, slaknesse, and excusacioun, and with ydelnesse and unlust, for which the book
seith: 'acursed be he that doth the service of god necli-
gently.'/ Thanne is Accidie enemy to everich estaat of
man; for certes, the estaat of man is in three maneres./
Outher it is th'estaat of innocence, as was th'estaat of
Adam biforn that he fil into sinne; in which estaat he was
holden to wirche, as in heryinge and adouringe of god./   20
Another estaat is the estaat of sinful men, in which estaat
men been holden to laboure in preyinge to god for
amendement of hir sinnes, and that he wole graunte hem
to arysen out of hir sinnes./ Another estaat is th'estaat of
grace, in which estaat he is holden to werkes of penitence;
and certes, to alle thise thinges is Accidie enemy and
contrarie. For he loveth no bisinesse at al./ Now certes,
this foule sinne Accidie is eek a ful greet enemy to the
lyflode of the body; for it ne hath no purveaunce agayn
temporel necessitee; for it forsleweth and forsluggeth, and   30
destroyeth alle goodes temporeles by reccheleesnesse./

The fourthe thinge is, that Accidie is lyk to hem that been
in the peyne of helle, by-cause of hir slouthe and of hir
hevinesse; for they that been dampned been so bounde,
that they ne may neither wel do ne wel thinke./ Of
Accidie comth first, that a man is anoyed and encombred
for to doon any goodnesse, and maketh that god hath
abhominacion of swich Accidie, as seith seint Johan./

Now comth Slouthe, that wol nat suffre noon hardnesse
ne no penaunce. For soothly, Slouthe is so tendre, and so   40
delicat, as seith Salomon, that he wol nat suffre noon
hardnesse ne penaunce, and therfore he shendeth al that he
dooth./ Agayns this roten-herted sinne of Accidie and
Slouthe sholde men exercise hem-self to doon gode
werkes, and manly and vertuously cacchen corage wel
to doon; thinkinge that oure lord Jesu Crist quyteth
every good dede, be it never so lyte./ Usage of labour is a

greet thing; for it maketh, as seith seint Bernard, the laborer to have stronge armes and harde sinwes; and Slouthe maketh hem feble and tendre./ Thanne comth drede to biginne to werke any gode werkes; for certes, he that is enclyned to sinne, him thinketh it is so greet an empryse for to undertake to doon werkes of goodnesse,/ and casteth in his herte that the circumstaunces of goodnesse been so grevouse and so chargeaunt for to suffre, that he dar nat undertake to do werkes of goodnesse, as seith seint Gregorie./

Now comth wanhope, that is despeir of the mercy of god, that comth somtyme of to muche outrageous sorwe, and somtyme of to muche drede: imagininge that he hath doon so muche sinne, that it wol nat availlen him, though he wolde repenten him and forsake sinne: thurgh which despeir or drede he abaundoneth al his herte to every maner sinne, as seith seint Augustin./ Which dampnable sinne, if that it continue un-to his ende, it is cleped sinning in the holy gost./ This horrible sinne is so perilous, that he that is despeired, ther nis no felonye ne no sinne that he douteth for to do; as shewed wel by Judas./ Certes, aboven alle sinnes thanne is this sinne most displesant to Crist, and most adversarie./ Soothly, he that despeireth him is lyk the coward champioun recreant, that seith creant withoute nede. Allas! allas! nedeles is he recreant and nedeles despeired./ Certes, the mercy of god is evere redy to every penitent, and is aboven alle hise werkes./ Allas! can nat a man bithinke him on the gospel of seint Luk, 15., where-as Crist seith that 'as wel shal ther be joye in hevene upon a sinful man that doth penitence, as up-on nynety and nyne rightful men that neden no penitence?'/ Loke forther, in the same gospel, the joye and the feste of the gode man that hadde lost his sone, whan his sone with repentaunce was retourned to his fader./ Can they nat remembren hem

eek, that, as seith seint Luk *xxiii° capitulo*, how that the
theef that was hanged bisyde Jesu Crist, seyde: 'Lord,
remembre of me, whan thou comest in-to thy regne?'/
'For sothe,' seyde Crist, 'I seye to thee, to-day shaltow
been with me in Paradys.'/ Certes, ther is noon so
horrible sinne of man, that it ne may, in his lyf, be
destroyed by penitence, thurgh vertu of the passion and
of the deeth of Crist./ Allas! what nedeth man thanne to   90
been despeired, sith that his mercy so redy is and large?
Axe and have./ Thanne cometh Sompnolence, that is,
sluggy slombringe, which maketh a man be hevy and dul,
in body and in soule; and this sinne comth of Slouthe./
And certes, the tyme that, by wey of resoun, men sholde
nat slepe, that is by the morwe; but-if ther were cause
resonable./ For soothly, the morwetyde is most covenable,
a man to seye his preyeres, and for to thinken on god,
and for to honoure god, and to yeven almesse to the
povre, that first cometh in the name of Crist./ Lo! what   100
seith Salomon: 'who-so wolde by the morwe awaken and
seke me, he shal finde.'/ Thanne cometh Necligence, or
recchelesnesse, that rekketh of no-thing. And how that
ignoraunce be moder of alle harm, certes, Necligence is
the norice./ Necligence ne doth no fors, whan he shal
doon a thing, whether he do it weel or baddely./

Of the remedie of thise two sinnes, as seith the wyse
man, that 'he that dredeth god, he spareth nat to doon
that him oghte doon.'/ And he that loveth god, he wol
doon diligence to plese god by his werkes, and abaundone   110
him-self, with al his might, wel for to doon./

HERE TAKETH THE MAKERE OF THIS BOOK HIS LEVE

Now preye I to hem alle that herkne this litel tretis or
rede, that if ther be any thing in it that lyketh hem, that
ther-of they thanken oure lord Jesu Crist, of whom

procedeth al wit and al goodnesse./ And if ther be any
thing that displese hem, I preye hem also that they
arrette it to the defaute of myn unconninge, and nat to my
wil, that wolde ful fayn have seyd bettre if I hadde had
conninge./ For oure boke seith, 'al that is writen is
writen for oure doctrine'; and that is myn entente./
Wherfore I biseke yow mekely for the mercy of god, that   10
ye preye for me, that Crist have mercy on me and foryeve
me my giltes:/—and namely, of my translacions and
endytinges of worldly vanitees, the whiche I revoke in my
retracciouns:/ as is the book of Troilus; The book also
of Fame; The book of the nynetene Ladies; The book of
the Duchesse; The book of seint Valentynes day of the
Parlement of Briddes; The tales of Caunterbury, thilke
that sounen in-to sinne;/ The book of the Leoun; and many
another book, if they were in my remembrance; and many
a song and many a lecherous lay; that Crist for his grete   20
mercy foryeve me the sinne./ But of the translacion of
Boece de Consolacione, and othere bokes of Legendes of
seintes, and omelies, and moralitee, and devocioun,/ that
thanke I oure lord Jesu Crist and his blisful moder, and
alle the seintes of hevene;/ bisekinge hem that they from
hennesforth, un-to my lyves ende, sende me grace to
biwayle my giltes, and to studie to the salvacioun of my
soule:—and graunte me grace of verray penitence,
confessioun and satisfaccioun to doon in this
present lyf;/ thurgh the benigne grace of him that is king   30
of kinges and preest over alle preestes, that boghte us
with the precious blood of his herte;/ so that I may been
oon of hem at the day of dome that shulle be saved:
Qui cum patre, &c.

*Here is ended the book of the Tales of Caunterbury, compiled by
Geffrey Chaucer, of whos soule Jesu Crist have mercy. Amen.*

APPENDICES

I. *ON READING CHAUCER*

Chaucer's verse is not difficult to read, and there is little point in attempting to 'modernize' him, quite apart from the fact that it is virtually impossible to do so. Manly remarks very pertinently that "the general principles of stress and movement in Chaucer's language and in his verse-patterns are, so far as we can discover, essentially the same as for Present English."

But one difference must be noted, and that is that a great many of his words ended in an unstressed final -*e*, -*en*, or -*es*. Moreover, a great number of his lines ended in feminine or double rhymes—a stressed syllable followed by one without stress.

The practical application of this is that the final -*e* of any Chaucerian line must always be pronounced, together with many other final syllables within the line itself, if the verse is to scan. Chaucer was a most subtle and careful craftsman, and it is certain that in practice many final syllables were either slurred or suppressed altogether. But the student who is prepared to give a little time to the practice of reading Chaucer aloud, giving the words their natural stresses, will soon get the feel of the verse, whether the line contains eleven syllables:

> Hath in the Ram his halfe cours y-ronne,

or ten:

> A Knyght ther was, and that a worthy man,

or nine:

> Twenty bookes clad in blak or reed.

In the Prologue, for example, the 'normal' line contains eleven syllables, and when this is understood the rest should come easily, though it must be admitted that long practice and considerable experience may be necessary before all the subtleties of Chaucer's practice can be recognized.

"All of Chaucer's narrative verse except the Monk's Tale is written either in rhymed couplets or in stanzas of seven lines. The rhymed couplet is his favourite form for both decasyllabic and octosyllabic verse." (Manly, *Canterbury Tales*, p. 131.)

II. *CHAUCER'S VOCABULARY*

The translator of Chaucer is obliged to keep three aspects of his language constantly in mind. Most of his words and phrases, of course, look—and are—modern. They present no particular difficulty to the ordinary reader, and that is why he can still be read easily and with pleasure after a minimum of preliminary inquiry.

On the other hand, a certain portion of his vocabulary is now completely obsolete. It has disappeared from common use, together with the things it describes. The reader faced by such words as *tombestere, habergeoun, anlas,* and *vernicle* has nothing to help him: he must perforce turn at once to the glossary.

But the main difficulty lies in those words which at first sight seem modern enough, but are often nothing of the kind. Sometimes their sense has changed completely since the fourteenth century. Sometimes the alteration has been only slight. At other times they are used with a connotation which is both medieval and modern.

Daunger, for example, is not 'danger' but 'control,' or 'power,' or 'disdain.' *Vileinye* is not 'villainy' but 'ill-breeding'; *lust* not 'lust,' but 'pleasure' or 'delight.' *Corage* usually means 'heart' or 'mind,' but it sometimes means 'courage'; *compleynen* is both to 'complain' and to 'lament.' And so on. It would be easy to compile a long list of similar examples. But perhaps enough has been said to show that there are times when only the student of some experience can hope to recognize the precise significance and appreciate the delightful subtlety of what Chaucer has in mind. And it is, at any rate, partly for this reason that the study of his work continues to exert so beguiling and perennial a fascination.

See, for an admirable survey, Manly, *Canterbury Tales*, pp. 88–122. Chaucer's English is the East Midland dialect (later to become what we now know as Standard English), as it was spoken in fourteenth-century London and at Court. He did not invent it, though he greatly increased its prestige and popularity by his writings, and demonstrated its suitability for every literary purpose. It was a language more highly inflected than modern English, but many of these inflections were dying out even as Chaucer was writing, and by the middle of the following century few, if any, clearly understood the secrets of his scansion, as a glance at Lydgate or Hoccleve will readily show. Very briefly, the following are some points worth noting:

Nouns. Many nouns have in the nominative case a final *-e* which has disappeared from modern English—*e.g.*, *endë*, *namë*.

The usual endings of nouns are as follows:

	Singular	*Plural*	
Nom. Acc.		*-es*	These endings are
Gen.	*-es*	*-es*	syllables, as a rule.
Dat.	*-e*	*-es*	

A few nouns have plurals in *-en* or *-n*: *brethren*, *toon* (toes), *fon* (foes), *asshen* (ashes). Some plurals are without endings: *deer*, *freend* (friends). The genitive singular is sometimes without ending. In *his lady grace*, "lady" is a relic of the old weak genitive in *-an*. The dative singular is inflected with *-e*, but often it is without ending.

Adjectives. Chaucer has two forms, strong and weak. The latter, ending in *-e*, is seen in *the yonge sonne*. It is also formed in connexion with nouns in the vocative, and with proper names. Uninflected adjectives usually end in a consonant; so do adjectives of two or more syllables. The plural ends in *-e*. The old genitive plural *-ra*, appears in *aller*— *e.g.*, *hir aller cappe* (the caps of them all).

Comparatives and superlatives are more or less what they are in modern English, *-er* and *-est*. But where *t* is the medial consonant it is doubled: gretter (greater).

Adverbs end in *-e*, *-ly*, or *-liche*. A few end in *-es*, or *-en*: ones (once), hennes (hence), aboven (above).

Pronouns are what they are now, with the exception of the third person plural: they, hir (their), and hem (them).

Verbs.

Strong verbs form their past tenses and past participles by changing the root vowel.

Speken: to speak

		Present			*Past*
Sing.	1.	speke	Sing.	1.	spak
	2.	spekest		2.	spak(e)
	3.	speketh		3.	spak
Plural.		speke(n)	Plural.		speken

Pres. Subj. Sing.: speke; Plural: speke(n).
Pres. Part.: speking(e).
Past Part.: y-spoken (y represents the Anglo-Saxon ge-) and spoken.
The Present Imperative plural ends in *-eth*.

Weak verbs form their past tenses by adding *-ed(e)* or *-de*, *-te* to the root, and their past participles by adding *-ed*, *-d*, or *t*.

Make(n): to make

		Present			*Past*
Sing.	1.	make	Sing.	1.	made
	2.	makest		2.	madest
	3.	maketh		3.	maked or made
Plural:		make(n)	Plural:		makeden or maden

Pres. Subj. Sing.: make; Plural: make(n).
Pres. Part.: making(e) or makying(e).
Past. Part.: y-maked, maked, or maad.
Present Imp. Sing.: make; Plural: maketh.

Strong-weak verbs. The present tense of these is an old strong past tense. The past tense is weak, ending in *-de* or *-te*.

		Present			Past
Sing.	1.	shal	Sing.	1.	sholde
	2.	shalt		2.	sholdest
	3.	shal		3.	sholde
Plural:		shull(en), shal	Plural:		sholde(n)

Impersonal verbs dispense with the implied subject 'it': *as him liste* (as it pleases, pleased, him). 'As' is often used for 'as if': *as it were a mede* (as though it were a meadow), or in the sense of modern 'as' or 'like.' It also introduces an adverbial phrase: *as of so litel space* (in such a short time).

NOTES

To Rosemounde. A Balade (p. 64)

This ballade was probably written somewhere about 1390. Some have thought it to be a satirical comment on the conventional love poem, and it cannot be denied that the barrel of tears and the soused pike are not very lover-like images. But see C. S. Lewis, *The Allegory of Love*, p. 171.

l. 2. mappemounde. *Mappa mundi*, the map of the world. A copy of a medieval *mappa mundi* is still preserved in Hereford Cathedral.

l. 20. Tristam. The Sir Tristram, or Tristan, of French medieval romance, lover of Bele Isolde, and a famous example of constancy.

Truth (p. 65)

This ballade, the noblest of Chaucer's short poems, was probably written between 1386 and 1390. The theme was possibly suggested to him by his reading of Boëthius, but there is no need to search hard for the source of an idea which he was perfectly capable of finding for himself. The poem was almost certainly addressed to Sir Philip de la Vache (see l. 22), the son-in-law of Chaucer's friend Sir Lewis Clifford. It was Clifford who in 1386 came home from France with Deschamps' famous ballade.

l. 3. climbing. Here perhaps in the sense of ambition.

l. 6. Werk. Robinson: *Reule*.

l. 7. shal delivere. Robinson: *thee shal delivere*, throughout.

l. 8. Do not distress yourself by attempting to put the world right.

l. 9. of hir that turneth as a bal. Fortune, the fickle goddess, who is often depicted standing on a wheel or globe.

l. 12. An allusion to Æsop's fable of the earthen and brazen pots.

l. 20. the hye wey. The main road; the sure road to your destination.

Chaucers Wordes unto Adam, his Owne Scriveyn (p.66)

This poem was probably written about 1386, and it is an interesting and amusing illustration of one of the difficulties which confronted authors in the fourteenth century. We do not know who

Adam was; possibly he was one of the clerks in Chaucer's office, though he is more likely to have been a professional scribe. These men too had their troubles: see H. S. Bennett, *The Pastons and their England* (Cambridge, 1922), pp. 112–113, for a somewhat pathetic specimen of the brotherhood.

l. 2. Boece. Boëthius, whose *De Consolatione Philosophiæ* Chaucer translated.

l. 3. lokkes. Robinson: *long lokkes*. The meaning is perhaps that Chaucer will hit him over the head, and thus cause a "scalle," or scab.

l. 4. trewe. Robinson: *more trewe*.

l. 6. rubbe and scrape. No doubt Adam had been writing on vellum or parchment, making a fair copy from Chaucer's draft.

The Romaunt of the Rose (pp.66–69)

(This extract corresponds to ll. 21–134 in the "Oxford Standard Authors" edition of Chaucer's works.)

In the Prologue to *The Legend of Good Women* Chaucer himself refers to his translation of the *Roman de la Rose*:

> For in pleyn text, with-outen nede of glose,
> Thou hast translated the Romaunce of the Rose.

So speaks the God of Love, accusing the poet of "heresy" against his law. (Prologue B, ll. 328–329.)

For an account of the poem see the introductory essay, pp. 21–26, and R. D. French, *A Chaucer Handbook* (1947), pp. 75–82. This translation, the only Middle English version of the *Roman de la Rose* in existence, was probably written about 1380. Chaucer's authorship has been disputed, but it is now generally agreed that at least the first 1,705 lines are his. See F. N. Robinson, *The Complete Works of Geoffrey Chaucer*, pp. 988–989.

ll. 22–23. The identity of the lady—if she is anything more than a conventional figure—is unknown. Chaucer is following de Lorris here.

l. 78. aguiler. Needle-case. Robinson notes that the word does not exist elsewhere in English.

queynt y-nogh. Elaborate; highly ornamented.

l. 84. "The sleeves were tightly laced or sewn with a thread"—Robinson.

l. 98. Seine. The river Seine.

l. 99. straighter wel away. A great deal wider.

The Boke of the Duchesse (pp. 69–74)

(This extract corresponds to ll. 62–220 in the "Oxford Standard Authors" edition of Chaucer's works.)

This poem, which Robinson describes as "not only the earliest, but almost the only production of Chaucer that can with confidence be attached to an actual occurrence," was probably written soon after 1369. Blanche of Lancaster, the wife of John of Gaunt, died in that year, and the poem was designed as a tribute to her memory and a compliment to the Duke.

l. 4. Alcyone. The story of Ceyx and Alcione is found in Ovid, *Metamorphoses*, xi, ll. 410 and following, and it appears also in Machaut's *Dit de la Fontaine Amoureuse*.

l. 27. eest and west. Everywhere.

l. 40. she. Robinson: *this lady*.

l. 93. his. In Ovid the messenger is Iris, the goddess of the rainbow. She is often described as the special messenger of Hera, or Juno: Callimachus represents her as sleeping under her throne, like a dog. See H. J. Rose, in *The Oxford Classical Dictionary*, 1949, "Iris."

l. 106. Eclympasteyre. It is difficult to be certain who this is—the name seems to be an invention of Chaucer's—but he is likely to be Icelon, the son of Morpheus, god of Sleep.

l. 146. at whiche. Robinson: *for such*.

l. 152. A!. Robinson: *Allas!*

The Parlement of Foules (pp. 74–82)

(This extract corresponds to ll. 378–623 in the "Oxford Standard Authors' edition of Chaucer's works.)

The Parlement of Foules was probably written soon after 1380, and though it is an example of a popular medieval *genre*, the love-debate, it may refer directly to contemporary events, notably the betrothal of Richard II and Anne of Bohemia in 1381. But nothing is certain, and most explanations of the allegory which have been offered contain insurmountable difficulties. See Robinson, *op. cit.* pp. 900–902.

Other medieval poets had made use of the device of a council of birds; Oton de Graunson, for example, describes a similar gathering on St Valentine's Day, and Chaucer was indebted to the *De Planctu Naturæ* of Alanus de Insulis for a few details—*e.g.*, the description of Nature as God's *vicaire* in l. 1. But his treatment of the theme is characteristically his own.

l. 2. hoot, cold. . . An allusion to the famous doctrine of the four 'humours' of the human body, the four elementary qualities: blood (hot and moist), phlegm (cold and moist), yellow bile (hot and dry), and black bile (cold and dry). These 'humours' had to be kept in equilibrium if perfect health were to be enjoyed. Chaucer alludes more than once to this theory, notably in *The Nun's Priest's Tale*, ll. 125–149. See also the Prologue, l. 333.

l. 8. seynt Valentynes day. There is more than one St Valentine, but not a great deal is known about any of them. The earliest saint of that name was executed on February 14, A.D. 269, during the reign of the emperor Claudius Gothicus. The association of the lovers' festival with St Valentine seems to be due to the fact that the feast of the saint falls in early spring: there is, so far, nothing else to account for it. See Brand's *Popular Antiquities* of *Great Britain*, "Faiths and Folklore," edited by W. Carey Hazlitt, 2 vols. (London, 1905), "St Valentine's Day."

l. 77. allone. Robinson: *fullonge*.

l. 129. take the charge. Robinson: *take on the charge*.

l. 133. as good. Robinson: *as fayr*.

The Hous of Fame (pp 82–85)

(This extract corresponds to ll. 529–660 in the "Oxford Standard Authors" edition of Chaucer's works.)

THE STORY

Book I: Chaucer begins by turning over in his mind the subject of dreams: what they are, and what causes them. He then describes how he himself, "the tenth day of December," dreamed that he was in a temple of glass, dedicated to Venus, upon the walls of which was depicted the story of Æneas, and in particular the sad fate of Dido. Leaving the temple, he finds himself in a sandy waste, and as he looks about him a golden eagle suddenly swoops down and carries him off.

Book II: The eagle tells him that as a reward for his long service in the cause of Love he is to be taken to the House of Fame, where he will hear tidings of lovers to his heart's content, for all earthly rumours fly there at once. The reason for this the eagle explains scientifically and at length, pointing out that since all things tend to move towards their appointed destinations, sound, which is broken air, naturally flies upwards to the House of Fame. The eagle then offers to teach Chaucer some astronomy, but the poet will have none of it. Meanwhile they have been flying up through the heavens, and at last they see before them the House of Fame. Putting Chaucer down *in a strete*, the eagle leaves him.

Book III: Chaucer finds that the House of Fame stands on a mountain of ice, upon which are carved the melting names of many who were once known in the world, and others whose reputation and names are still fresh. He climbs up with great difficulty, and arrives at a magnificent palace, full of suitors who have come to ask favour of the goddess. Some wish for fame; others desire oblivion. But Fame is capricious, and many are given the opposite of what they seek. After he has watched the proceedings for a while he is led by a somewhat mysterious bystander to a house of twigs, made by Dædalus, and continually spinning. Here all rumours collect and grow in size, passing from mouth to mouth. The eagle has by this time appeared again, and agreed that Chaucer shall be given time to observe the wonders of the place. At length he is aware of the presence of 'a man of great authority,' and at this point the poem comes to an abrupt end.

The Hous of Fame was probably written somewhere between 1374 and 1385, when Chaucer was Controller of Customs and Subsidy of Wools, Skins, and Hides in the Port of London. This seems clear from the words of the eagle in Book II, ll. 652–658:

> For whan thy labour doon al is,
> And hast y-maad thy rekeninges,
> In stede of reste and newe thinges,
> Thou gost hoom to thy hous anoon;
> And, also domb as any stoon,
> Thou sittest at another boke,
> Til fully daswed is thy loke.

But it has so far been found impossible to date the poem with any degree of precision. For an account of Chaucer's sources, and other relevant material, see Robinson, *op. cit.* pp. 886–888.

l. 5. hir beautee. Robinson: *the beaute*.

l. 45. Seynte Marie. Compare *The Parlement of Foules*, l. 72, where the tercel *of lower kinde* swears by St John.

l. 58. stellifye. Make into a constellation, as were Hercules, Perseus, and Andromeda.

l. 60. Enok. Chaucer refers here to several famous examples of sudden translation to Heaven.

For Enoch see Genesis v, 24: ". . . and he was not, for God took him."

Elye is Elijah (II Kings ii, 11).

Romulus was carried to heaven by Mars; Ganymede (on account of his great beauty) by Jupiter, in the form of an eagle.

l. 64. boteler. Butler. Ganymede was made cupbearer to the gods.

l. 71. as yet. A characteristic Chaucerian touch.

Troilus and Criseyde (pp. 86–103)

THE STORY

Book I: Calkas of Troy, a seer, deserts to the Greeks, leaving his daughter Criseyde in the city. Troilus, the son of Priam, King of Troy, sees her in the Temple of Pallas, and, though he had hitherto scoffed at love, he is at once overwhelmed by her beauty and charm. His passion increases with every day that follows, and in the end he confides in his friend Pandarus, Criseyde's uncle, who promises to help him.

Book II: Pandarus visits Criseyde, who is timid and fearful, and persuades her to look kindly on Troilus. When he has gone Troilus rides past her window and makes a deep impression on her heart. Pandarus now insists that Troilus shall write Criseyde a letter, which he delivers next morning. While they are talking together Troilus again rides by. Pandarus persuades Deiphebus to invite Criseyde to dinner to meet Hector, Paris, Helen, and Troilus, so that she shall not suffer by her father's treachery. Troilus is to go beforehand and pretend to be ill. After dinner, when the others have left him, Criseyde and Pandarus visit Troilus, and he is able to declare his love for Criseyde.

Book III: Criseyde agrees to consider Troilus as her knight. They now meet frequently. Pandarus invites Criseyde to dinner at his house and conceals Troilus in an upper room. Heavy rain prevents Criseyde from going home, and she agrees to stay the night. Later Pandarus brings Troilus to her room.

Book IV: A temporary truce is arranged between the Trojans and the Greeks, and Calkas, in return for his services, asks for Criseyde in exchange for the Trojan warrior Antenor, captured in a skirmish. This is agreed to, in spite of the opposition of Hector. The lovers are distracted with grief, but Criseyde promises to return within ten days.

Book V: Criseyde is escorted to the Greek camp by Diomede.

Troilus, in great misery, counts the days and revisits the scenes of his former happiness. Meanwhile, Diomede lays siege to Criseyde, and succeeds in winning her love. Troilus finally realizes that he has been betrayed. He seeks to kill Diomede in battle, but without success. In the end he is himself killed by Achilles.

Troilus and Criseyde was probably written between 1385 and 1387. For Chaucer's treatment of his sources see the introductory essay, pp. 45–48, Robinson, *op. cit.*, pp. 449–453, and pp. 922–924; French, *op. cit.*, pp. 135–191.

Chaucer himself says that his immediate authority was one "Lollius": nowhere does he mention either Boccaccio or *Il Filostrato*. But Lollius is still a mystery. It is possible that Chaucer had in mind the Lollius addressed by Horace:

> Troiani belli scriptorem, maxime Lolli.
> (*Epistles*, I, ii, *l*. 1)

Still, there seems no reason why Chaucer should have transferred Boccaccio's rights to him. It may be that he simply wished to pay Boccaccio a compliment by identifying him (however mistakenly) with a writer on the Trojan War honoured by such a poet as Horace. Or again, he may have liked to pretend that he had something better than a modern authority for his story.

The poem was revised from time to time, and Chaucer possibly intended to work at it still further. See French, *op. cit.*, pp. 190–191, and R. K. Root, *Troilus and Criseyde* (Princeton, 1926).

TROILUS SEES CRISEYDE FOR THE FIRST TIME (p. 86)

(This extract corresponds to ll. 183–280 (Book I) in the "Oxford Standard Authors" edition of Chaucer's work.)

l. 28. ". . . the very greatness of the man, his seeming security, and his jeering diatribes against love are no protection. The god smites whom he will: the great warrior falls, and once smitten his behaviour is axiomatic."—H. S. Bennett, *Chaucer and the Fifteenth Century*, p. 54. Robinson observes that these cynical remarks of Troilus are taken from *Il Filostrato* and possibly represent Boccaccio's own opinions.

l. 36. Bayard. The name of the horse given by Charlemagne to Renaud.

Pandarus pays Criseyde a Visit (p. 89)

(*This extract corresponds to ll. 50–147 (Book II) in the "Oxford Standard Authors" edition of Chaucer's works.*)

l. 6. Bole. The zodiacal sign Taurus, the Bull.

l. 15. Proignè. Procne, the wife of Tereus and sister of Philomela. The gods changed her into a swallow, and her sister into a nightingale, as a result of the outrage done to Philomela by Tereus.

l. 25. An allusion to the medieval (and modern) practice of making astrological calculations before undertaking any important task, or going a journey. *Cf.* the Doctor in the Prologue with his *houres* and *magik naturel*.

l. 28. Janus. The most ancient of the Roman gods, who presided over all going out and coming in, all places of entrance and passage, and all doors and gates. He was represented with two faces looking in opposite directions. In time of war the doors of his temple were always open.

l. 35. The famous story of the Siege of Thebes, for which the *Thebaid* of Statius was Chaucer's classical authority. It was divided into *bokes twelve*; l. 59.

l. 52. Laius. King of Thebes, and father of Œdipus, who unwittingly killed him and married his mother Jocasta, who later hanged herself.

l. 54. A purely medieval touch. In manuscripts the section headings are often written in red.

l. 55. bisshop. Priest.

l. 56. Amphiorax. Amphiaraus, son of Oecles (or Apollo). "He attacked Thebes at the Homoloian Gate, was driven off, and, as he fled, was swallowed up in a cleft in the ground made by Zeus' thunderbolt." H. J. Rose, in *The Oxford Classical Dictionary*.

l. 61. barbe. Root: *wympel*.

Antigone's Song (p. 93)

(*This extract corresponds to ll. 813–924 (Book II) in the "Oxford Standard Authors" edition of Chaucer's works.*)

l. 4. Flexippe. The origin of the names of Criseyde's nieces is unknown.

ll. 8–10. A description of a typical medieval garden.

l. 48. him. Root: *it*.

l. 55. "Those who live in glass houses shouldn't throw stones."
l. 86. Criseyde changes the subject with a trivial remark, "Dear me, it's getting late."
ll. 92–93. Chaucer may be poking fun at himself (and at conventional poets) here. But, as so often happens, it is impossible to be certain.
ll. 96–97. Possibly this is a reminiscence of Virgil, Æneid VI, ll. 271–272: ". . . ubi caelum condidit umbra Iuppiter, et rebus nox abstulit atra colorem."

TROILUS LAMENTS THE LOSS OF HIS FORMER HAPPINESS (p. 96)

(This extract corresponds to ll. 519–630 (Book V) in the "Oxford Standard Authors" edition of Chaucer's works.)

l. 19. forth bigan. Root, Robinson: *forthby gan.*
l. 45. forth by. Root, Robinson: *forby.*
l. 47. Root, Robinson. *Lo, yonder saugh ich last my lady daunce.*
l. 83. A reference, from Statius, to the anger of Juno against Athamas. Because Ino, the wife of Athamas, had nursed Dionysus, Hera (Juno) drove both her and her husband mad. See H. J. Rose, in *The Oxford Classical Dictionary*: "Athamas."

THE END OF THE STORY (p. 99)

(This extract corresponds to ll. 1750–1869 (Book V) in the "Oxford Standard Authors" edition of Chaucer's works.)

l. 7. Diomede. Diomedes, son of Tydeus and Deipyle. He took a prominent part in the Trojan War, and is represented as both wise and courageous. Among his exploits were the wounding of Aphrodite and Ares, and the killing of Rhesus in a raid on the Trojan camp with Odysseus.
l. 42. Lucan. Marcus Annæus Lucanus, A.D. 39–65, author of the *Bellum Civile* or *Pharsalia*, a poem in ten books mainly concerned with the war between Cæsar and Pompey.
l. 52. thousandes. According to Guido delle Colonne, Troilus on one occasion slew a thousand men.
l. 60. In convers letinge. Leaving on the other side, leaving behind.
l. 62. The erratik sterres. The planets.
armonye. The music of the spheres. See *The Merchant of Venice*, Act V, Sc. 1, ll. 60–62.
l. 77. One of Mercury's duties was to guide the spirits of the dead.
l. 99. Payens. Pagans.

l. 103. rascaille. This is a strangely ungenerous epithet for Chaucer to apply to the deities of the ancient world, in whom he had taken such delight for so many years. But here he is in that sober and pious mood which with him was never far below the surface.

l. 106. moral Gower. John Gower, Chaucer's fellow-poet and friend, who has been "moral Gower" ever since. Chaucer has of course no humorous intent; he is paying his friend a sincere compliment and calling attention to the elevated—and elevating—character of his writings.

l. 107. Strode. Ralph Strode, Fellow of Merton College, Oxford, distinguished as a logician and an opponent of Wycliffe.

l. 118. grace. Root, Robinson: *mercy*.

The Legend of Good Women (pp. 103–111)

(This extract corresponds to ll. 1–269, Text B, in the "Oxford Standard Authors" edition of Chaucer's works.)

This poem was probably written between 1386 and 1395, and almost certainly at the request of Queen Anne, the wife of Richard II. There are twelve MSS. in existence, though some of these are fragmentary. The Prologue exists in two versions, known as A and B. The A text is found in only one MS., now in the Cambridge University Library, and is generally considered to be the later version, since a dedication to Anne, found in the B text, is omitted:

> And whan this book is maad, yive it the quene,
> On my behalfe, at Eltham, or at Shene.
> *Text B, ll. 496–497*

The Queen died in 1394, and Chaucer may well have thought that these lines might cause pain to the King, who was heart-broken at his loss, and caused the palace at Sheen—Anne's favourite residence —to be pulled down.

This prologue, it may be noted, contains one of the loveliest of all Chaucer's ballades:

> "Hyd, Absolon, thy gilte tresses clere."
> B text, ll. 249–269.

l. 16. Bernard. Probably St Bernard of Clairvaux (1091–1153). The Latin form of the proverb is, "Bernardus monachus non vidit omnia."

l. 43. daysies. Without wishing to take anything from the charm of this famous passage, it must be pointed out that the cult of the daisy, or marguerite, was a fourteenth-century convention, borrowed from France, where Deschamps, Machaut, and Froissart had all subscribed to it. See J. L. Lowes, *Convention and Revolt in Poetry* (London, 1930), pp.36–39.

l. 69. make of sentement. Write poems about the feelings. The passage is addressed to Chaucer's contemporaries among the 'makers.'

l. 72. It seems likely that Court circles in England and France were divided into two parties, one devoted to the Flower and the other to the Leaf, denoting respectively Beauty and Constancy. An early fifteenth-century poem, *The Flower and the Leaf*, was for long attributed to Chaucer himself.

l. 74. You have reaped the field of poetry and carried away the harvest.

l. 114. Agenores doghter. Europa, who was carried off by Jupiter in the form of a bull.

l. 120. The daisy of course has no scent, and Chaucer is here following the example of the marguerite poets, who transferred this attribute of the rose to the daisy. See Lowes, *op. cit.*, pp. 36–37.

l. 145. seynt Valentyn. See the note to l. 8 of *The Parlement of Foules*.

l. 160. Daunger. Here used in the sense of disdain, fastidiousness.

l. 166. Etik. This word is something of a puzzle—it might refer either to a book or a person. Skeat's view was that the reference is to the *Ethics* of Aristotle, in which the doctrine of the Mean is promulgated. Virtue lies in the balance between two extremes. Robinson notes that the epithet is often applied to Horace by John of Salisbury, and suggests that the quotation is from a paraphrase of the Epistles in his *Policraticus*.

l. 171. Zephirus. God of the West Wind, sometimes described as the husband of Iris (see the note to l. 93 of *The Boke of the Duchesse*).

Flora. The goddess of flowering or blossoming plants.

l. 196. thing. Robinson: *stryf*.

l. 249. Absolon. Absalom, son of David, and famous for the beauty of his long hair, which in the end caused his death. See II Samuel xviii, 9–17.

l. 251. Jonathas. Jonathan, the friend of David. Together they are an often-quoted example of constancy in friendship. See I Samuel xix, 1.

l. 252. Penalopee. Penelope, the wife of Odysseus. She waited twenty years for his return from his wanderings, in spite of the importunity of her many suitors.

Marcia Catoun. Marcia, the wife of Cato Uticensis.

l. 257. Lavyne. Lavinia, the daughter of Latinus. She was betrothed to Turnus, but on his death she was given in marriage to Æneas.

Lucresse. Lucrece (Lucretia), the wife of L. Tarquinius Collatinus. Her story is best known from Shakespeare's poem, *The Rape of Lucrece*.

l. 258. Polixene. Polyxena, the daughter of Priam and Hecuba.

l. 261. Tisbe. Thisbe. The story of Pyramus and Thisbe is now best known from the play performed by the mechanicals in *A Midsummer Night's Dream*.

l. 263. Herro. Hero, priestess of Aphrodite at Sestos, on the Hellespont. Her lover Leander used to swim across to her from Abydos, but one night he was drowned in a storm, and Hero in despair threw herself into the sea.

Laodameia, the wife of Protesilaus, a prince of Thessaly. He was killed as he leapt ashore at Troy, and Laodameia was so griefstricken that the gods allowed him to return to her for three hours. When he left her again she killed herself.

l. 264. Phyllis. The daughter of the Thracian king Sithon. She was to have been married to Demophon, son of Theseus and Phaedra, but he went to Attica and stayed away so long that Phyllis thought she had been forgotten and hanged herself.

l. 265. Canace. The daughter of Æolus who committed incest with her brother Macareus.

l. 266. Ysiphile. Hypsipyle, daughter of Thoas, King of Lemnos, whose life she saved when the Lemnian women massacred all the men of the island. The Argonauts landed on Lemnos, and stayed there for a year. During this period Hypsipyle bore twins to Jason, their leader.

l. 268. Ypermistre. Hypermnestra, daughter of Danaus, who spared her husband Lynceus when her father, who had fifty daughters, ordered them to kill their husbands, the sons of Ægyptus, on their wedding night.

Adriane. Ariadne, daughter of Minos of Crete, who saved Theseus from the Minotaur by giving him a thread with which he was able to find his way out of the Labyrinth.

The Canterbury Tales (pp. 111–154)

THE PROLOGUE (pp. 111–136)

(This extract corresponds to the complete text in the "Oxford Standard Authors" edition of Chaucer's works.)

The Prologue was probably composed somewhere about 1387, and completed before the majority of the Tales were written, though it seems likely that it was revised from time to time, and that the Reeve, Miller, Summoner, Pardoner, Manciple, and Wife of Bath were added after the first draft was completed.

l. 5. Zephirus. The West Wind. See the note to l. 171 of *The Legend of Good Women*.

l. 6. Inspired. Quickened, breathed upon.

l. 8. the Ram. The sun has passed through the latter half of the zodiacal sign Aries and the first half of Taurus: therefore it is past the 11th of April and the sun is still "young."

l. 9. smale fowles. Manly remarks that Chaucer probably has nightingales in mind here.

l. 13. palmers. By Chaucer's time the term 'palmer' was synonymous with 'pilgrim,' but strictly speaking, a palmer was one who had been to the Holy Land and brought back a palm-branch as a token.

l. 17. martir. St Thomas à Becket, Archbishop of Canterbury, murdered in his cathedral in 1170. He was canonized in 1173.

l. 20. Tabard. A herald's coat, a representation of which would have been used as the inn-sign. There was an actual inn of this name in Southwark in Chaucer's time.

l. 47. his lordes werre. The King's service.

l. 51. Alisaundre. Alexandria, "won" (and abandoned) in 1365 by Pierre de Lusignan, King of Cyprus.

l. 52. He had presided at the head of the table.

l. 53. in Pruce. In Prussia, with the Teutonic Knights who were continually fighting the Russians and Lithuanians in *Ruce* and *Lettow*.

l. 56. Gernade. Granada.

l. 57. Algezir. Algeciras, taken from the Moorish King of Granada in 1344.

l. 57. *Belmarye* (Benmarin) and *Tramissene* (Tlemcen) were possessions of the Moors in Africa.

l. 58. Lyeys (Ayas) was captured from the Turks by Pierre de Lusignan in 1367.

Satalye (Attalia or Adalia) was also captured by de Lusignan, somewhere about 1352.

l. 59. the Grete See. The Mediterranean.

l. 60. aryve. Manly-Rickert, Robinson: *armee* (armed expedition by sea or land). This is almost certainly the correct reading.

l. 63. The Knight had successfully accepted three challenges to single combat.

l. 65. Palatye. Palathia in Anatolia, still held by the Christian Knights after the Turkish conquest of the area.

l. 74. hors. Plural. The Knight probably had two horses, one to ride and one to carry his baggage. Many of the great horses which carried the armoured knights of the Middle Ages came from the old French province of La Perche.

l. 75–78. fustian. Rough cloth.
gipoun. A tightly fitting coat or jerkin, which was stained, *bismotered*, with rust-marks from his *habergeoun*, or coat of chain-mail. The point is that in his pious haste to give thanks for his safe return he had not bothered to change into anything finer. As Chaucer says, he had just come back from abroad.

l. 79. Squyer. Esquire; one who attended a knight and carried his shield and lance.

l. 80. bacheler. An aspirant to knighthood. Compare the modern term Bachelor of Arts, used to describe those who may be said to be 'aspiring' towards a master's degree.

l. 81. leyd in presse. Artificially curled. But the Squire's hair was naturally curly.

l. 85. chivachye. Military expedition on horseback.

l. 88. This was traditional; an aspirant to knighthood without his lady would be unthinkable.

l. 89. Embrouded. In the Ellesmere manuscript the Squire is depicted wearing an embroidered coat and hat.

l. 95. He coude songes make. He could compose music.

l. 96. This is an interesting list of the accomplishments required of a gentleman in the fourteenth century. Chaucer himself was probably capable of performing all these activities.

l. 100. Ability to carve was essential in Chaucer's time; medieval people ate a great variety of meat and game.

l. 101. Yeman. The yeoman here is the personal servant of the knight on the pilgrimage, but back on the estate he no doubt had his own work to do as a *forster* (l. 117). His knowledge of "wood-craft" would be very valuable.

l. 104. Peacocks' feathers were widely used for arrow-flights in

Chaucer's time. But by 1545, when Roger Ascham published his *Toxophilus*, goose feathers seem to have superseded them in popularity.

l. 106. takel. Equipment.

l. 115. Cristofre. An image of St Christopher, the patron saint of travellers and foresters.

l. 118. Prioresse. She was no doubt the head of a small community attached to a large nunnery, and almost certainly a woman of good family, otherwise she would hardly have known anything about *chere of court*. It is worth noting that as a nun she had strictly no business to be on a pilgrimage at all, or any right to wear personal jewellery (l. 160), or to have a pleated wimple (l.151), or to keep dogs (l. 146), or to allow her forehead to be seen (ll. 154–155).

l. 120. sëynt Loy. St Eligius, Bishop of Noyon in the seventh century, the patron saint of goldsmiths and a man of great courtesy and personal beauty—in short, a very proper saint for a woman with the tastes of the Prioress to swear by. It has been suggested that since St Eligius objected to swearing, "to swear by St Loy" was equivalent to not swearing at all.

l.121. madame Eglentyne. "Lady Sweetbriar," the sort of pretty and romantic name one might expect this Prioress to have.

l. 123. in hir nose. This nasal intonation was customary in the performance of parts of the church services. It is still occasionally to be heard.

l. 124. Frensh. There has been a good deal of speculation on the subject of this joke, for joke it is. Some—Skeat, for example—have taken it as a plain statement of fact. The Prioress spoke French well, but it was the French she had learned at the Benedictine nunnery of St Leonard, near Stratford at Bow, and not the French of Paris. But this interpretation assumes that Chaucer thought that Stratford French was as good as Parisian French, which is manifestly absurd. He had good reason to know the difference. The remark is simply another amused comment on the Prioress's charming pretentiousness.

l. 127. An interesting picture of correct medieval table-manners, taken in this instance largely from the *Roman de la Rose*, but perfectly authentic, and illustrative of conditions in Chaucer's own day. People in the fourteenth century did not gnaw at huge bones and tear fowls apart in a frenzy, as some film-producers would have us believe.

ll. 152–156. These lines show that the Prioress is a typical medieval beauty, with her blue (not grey) eyes, straight nose, small red mouth, and beautiful wide forehead. If her hair had been visible it would undoubtedly have been golden; medieval English beauties are usually of what we call the 'Saxon' type. The impression is that of a small and delicate woman, but Chaucer says she was "nat undergrowe," which means, one supposes, that she was fairly tall.

l. 159. a peire of bedes. A rosary, with the Paternosters (the "gawdies," the larger beads) of green.

l. 160. This brooch was in the shape of a capital A surmounted by a crown. It is true that "Amor" can mean both heavenly and earthly love, but there seems little doubt that Chaucer has a mild joke in mind. And after all the observation is Virgil's in the first instance; *Eclogue* X, l. 69.

l. 165. a Monk. Like the Prioress, the Monk is thoroughly worldly, and cares nothing for the Rule which he had sworn to obey, and which in its earliest form demanded that he should stay in his cloister, fast and pray, and perform a regular daily task of manual labour. By Chaucer's time monks were often in the position of eighteenth-century Fellows of Oxford and Cambridge colleges, living very comfortably and with servants to attend to their wants.

l. 166. out-rydere. An official whose business it was to look after the estates belonging to the monastery. Monasteries were often very great landowners—as a result of pious benefactions—with property stretching far over the countryside.

l. 172. keper of the celle. A cell was a small monastery, dependent on a larger house, which might even be in another country. This monk, as the head of such a community, was probably a Prior. Chaucer says in fact that he was well qualified, in personal dignity, to hold the higher rank of Abbot.

l. 173. St Maur or Maurus was a disciple of St Benedict (or Benet), who drew up the first monastic Rule. St Benedict's central monastery was at Monte Cassino (destroyed in 1944), which was founded in 529.

l. 176. the space. Meanwhile, for the time being.

l. 177. a pulled hen. A plucked hen, something of no value, at any rate in the fourteenth century.

ll. 179–181. A well-known proverb: "Sicut piscis sine aqua caret vita, ita sine monasterio monachus."

l. 187. Austin. St Augustine of Hippo (A.D. 354–430), regarded by the Augustinian Canons as their founder.

l. 193. The Monk's habit richly trimmed with grey fur (gris) is another indication of his worldliness. Monks were forbidden to wear fine clothes.

l. 196. a curious pin. An elaborate brooch or pin, with a "love-knot," a complicated system of loops, at the head. It is perhaps not a coincidence that the Prioress's brooch should bear the motto *Amor vincit omnia* and the Monk's pin a love-knot.

l. 208. A Frere. There were four orders of Friars: the Dominicans, or Black Friars; the Franciscans, or Grey Friars; the Carmelites, or White Friars; and the Augustinian (or Austin) Friars. Friars, unlike monks, were commanded to go out into the world and preach the Gospel. They were forbidden to own property, and their personal possessions were to be confined to a cloak, a scrip, and a staff. They were to subsist on the gifts of the charitable, and they were to accept no money.

It is thus to be seen that there was a vast difference between Chaucer's Friar and the early disciples of St Francis, the founder of the first Order.

l. 209. limitour. A begging friar with his own 'limit,' or district: *cf.* the modern commercial traveller's 'round.'

ll. 212–213. He had found husbands for many of his discarded mistresses.

l. 214. *Cf.* the phrase: "a pillar of the church."

l. 220. He had his Order's licence to hear confession and grant absolution. This privilege often caused friction between parish priest and friar, quite apart from the friar's habit of taking money out of the parish in the form of alms.

l. 233. This practice of carrying round presents for distribution in the right quarter was much frowned upon by moralists, and contributed greatly to the later conception of the friar as a cheap trickster.

l. 245. lazars. Lepers. Leprosy was common during the Middle Ages, though the term was undoubtedly used to describe a variety of skin diseases.

l. 254. *In principio*. The opening words of St John's Gospel in the Vulgate:
"In principio erat verbum . . ."
Friars began their visits from house to house by quoting these words.

l. 256. What he picked up by begging on his own account was much more than his income.
The *rente* is perhaps the regular collection which he turned

M

over to his convent. The point is that he was out for his own profit.

l. 258. love-dayes. Days set apart for the settling of differences by arbitration. The Friar had acted as mediator on such occasions, as the clergy often did.

l. 261. maister. A Master of Arts, a person of considerable dignity in the Middle Ages.

pope. Perhaps a bishop or abbot, a person of great consequence: not the head of the Roman Church.

l. 263. the presse. The mould.

l. 270. forked berd. Forked beards were fashionable in Chaucer's time. He is wearing one himself in the Hoccleve portrait.

l. 271. mottelee. Motley, parti-coloured cloth; perhaps the livery of a guild. Manly explains it as "a rich cloth in which was woven a figured design, sometimes in the same color as the ground, sometimes in another."

l. 276. The Merchant wished the sea to be kept clear of pirates between Middelburg in Holland and the mouth of the river Orwell, near Harwich. The wool staple was at Middelburg from 1384 until 1388.

l. 278. sheeldes. Shields (crowns, Fr. *écus*), so called from the device of a shield stamped on them. They were worth between £2 and £3 in modern currency.

ll. 285–286. Clerk. A University student. This clerk was already a priest and a Bachelor of Arts, and was perhaps working for a higher degree.

Logic was one of the three subjects required for the Trivium, or preliminary examination. The other two were Grammar and Rhetoric.

l. 292. offyce. Secular employment. In the Middle Ages clerks and priests did much of the work now done by lawyers, schoolmasters, and accountants. Langland has much to say of priests who neglect their spiritual duties to engage in such mundane—and profitable—occupations.

l. 294. twenty bokes. A very considerable library in the Middle Ages, much larger than one would normally have expected to find even in a great house. Manuscripts were scarce and expensive, and few scholars had their own books. They were usually bound in leather (*blak or reed*) over wooden boards, but sometimes velvet or other material was used to cover them. Chaucer simply means that the Clerk loved learning better than leading a gay life. It is perhaps doubtful whether he actually had twenty books at the head of his bed: they would have been worth a small fortune in the fourteenth century, and we know that he was very poor. On the other hand, Chaucer says that he bought books with part of the money his friends gave him.

l. 297. This is one of Chaucer's happiest plays on words. 'Philosopher' was the term used to describe both a student of philosophy and a seeker after the 'Philosopher's Stone,' which would turn base metals into gold or silver.

l. 302. Many poor students supported themselves by begging if they were unable to come by the medieval equivalent of a scholarship or exhibition.

The terms 'sizar' at Cambridge and 'servitor' at Oxford are reminders of the days—still fairly recent—when poor scholars performed menial tasks in return for the means to *scoleye*.

l. 309. Sergeant. Serjeants were very distinguished lawyers: few had proceeded to this dignity. They were selected from barristers of sixteen years' standing, and from their ranks were drawn the justices of the King's court and the chief baron of the Exchequer.

l. 310. parvys. Perhaps the porch of St Paul's Cathedral, where lawyers used to meet to discuss business. But Manly suggests either "he had often sat in the court of the Exchequer," or "he had often presided at the moots of students in the inns of court," and prefers the latter explanation.

l. 315. patente. An open letter from the King appointing him a justice. pleyn commissioun. This allowed him to try all sorts of cases.

l. 317. robes. Presents of clothes, which were often very elaborate and expensive, were a recognized form of reward in the Middle Ages. The Man of Law had received his *robes* from grateful clients.

l. 320. purchasing. Conveyancing, the drawing up of deeds for the transfer of property.
infect. Invalid, without legal force.

Property held in 'fee simple' can be disposed of without restriction: if it is 'entailed' it cannot, but must go to a predetermined line of successors. The Man of Law was so clever that he could always get round this formidable difficulty and purchase the property, perhaps for himself.

l. 324. king William. William the Conqueror.

l. 331. Frankeleyn. A substantial landowner, a country squire.

l. 333. sangwyn. A reference to the doctrine of the four humours. See the note to *The Parlement of Foules*, l. 2. "Sanguine" people were of a hot and moist humour. *Complexioun* here does not refer to the Franklin's looks, but to his temperament. On the other hand, a "sanguine" person would be likely to have a ruddy face.

l. 334. sop. Pieces of bread or cake dipped in wine.

l. 336. Epicurus. The Greek philosopher (341–270 B.C.) who held that philosophy consisted in the wise conduct of life. His contention was that pleasure—or the absence of pain—is the only good, and that the best pleasure is a perfect harmony of body. But he advocated plain living, and the modern—Chaucer's—interpretation of an Epicurean as one devoted to sensuous enjoyment does not reflect the real teaching of Epicurus.

l. 340. Seint Julian. The patron saint of hospitality.

l. 342. no wher. Manly-Rickert: *neuere*.

l. 343. bake mete. Meat and fish pies.

l. 350. in stewe. "Stewes" were fish-ponds, of which there were a great many in medieval England. Some of them still exist. It is to be remembered that there were many fast-days when fish had to be eaten.

l. 352. poynaunt. Tasty. Sauces of all kinds were very popular, possibly owing to the tasteless nature of some of the food, particularly in winter. And something obviously had to be done with fish such as carp or pike.

l. 353. table dormant. Medieval tables were usually temporary structures, since the hall was the chief living-room in a manor-house. A table dormant was a table which was permanently in position, and the fact that the Franklin had one of these is an indication of his generosity. Food was always ready for any guest who might come in.

l. 355. sessiouns. Sessions of the Peace. The Franklin was what we should now call a J.P.

l. 356. knight of the shire. Member of Parliament for the county. Chaucer was Knight of the Shire for Kent in 1386.

l. 359. shirreve. Shire-reeve, the governor of a county, the modern Sheriff.

countour. An accountant, or possibly a pleader in court.

l. 360. vavasour. A vassal or tenant, one who held his land in fealty, possibly from some great lord. The feudal system was based on such tenancies.

363. liveree. They wore the livery or dress of a philanthropic or religious guild.

l. 370. deys. Dais, the raised platform at the end of the hall, where the high table was; the place of honour.

l. 372. alderman. Here the reference is to the head of the guild.

l. 377. vigilyës. Vigils were meetings held in churches—or church-yards—on the evenings before the great festivals.

l. 382. London ale was the best and most expensive. Medieval ale was brewed from malt, and did not contain hops, which were only introduced in the reign of Elizabeth.

l. 386. mormal. A cancerous growth or ulcer.

l. 389. Dertemouthe. Dartmouth is still a port, though it is much less important now than it was in Chaucer's time.

l. 395. a good felawe. Probably a contemptuous description—'a pretty rascal.'

l. 396. He had often stolen wine which he was carrying from Bordeaux under the very nose of the merchant to whom it belonged.

l. 400. He sent them home by water—threw them overboard. There is no suggestion here of 'walking the plank,' which was an elaborate and studied procedure designed to entertain the ship's company of a pirate vessel; or so we are told.

l. 404. Cartage. Probably Cartagena, or New Carthage, in Southeast Spain.

l. 408. Gootlond. Probably the island of Gotland, off the coast of Sweden. Visby, its capital, was an important trading town. But it is possible that Chaucer is referring to Jutland.

l. 409. Britayne. Brittany.

l. 410. Maudelayne. St Mary Magdalene. Medieval ships were often given the names of saints. Magdalene College, Cambridge, and Magdalen College, Oxford, are still called "Maudlin."

l. 414. astronomye. Astrology, *magik naturel*. l. 416.

l. 416. In houres. He watched for the ascendant of a favourable star, since the whole science depended (and depends) on the belief that the stars influence human life.

l. 418. images. These were either horoscopes or astrological talismans, or figures of the patient similar to the wax images used in witchcraft. The first explanation is much the more likely.

l. 420. Another allusion to the doctrine of the four humours. See l. 333.

l. 422. This line may be ironical, but, for all that, Chaucer's description of the doctor's methods is true to the facts, horrifying though they are. This is a fair description of a medieval physician: what a medieval surgeon was like is perhaps better left to the imagination. Surgery was in any case the despised sister of medicine.

ll. 429–434. These lines contain a list of famous authorities on the practice of medicine. Physicians based their practice on what

these men had written; there was little or no attempt to verify
their conclusions by experiment. The tyranny of the written word
in the Middle Ages is nowhere better exemplified than here.

Esculapius is Æsculapius, the legendary father of medicine,
Deiscorides is Dioscorides, a Greek writer on the *materia medica*
who lived about A.D. 50; *Rufus* is Rufus of Ephesus, who lived in
the second century; *Ypocras* is Hippocrates, the greatest of Greek
physicians, who was born at Cos about 460 B.C.; *Haly* is perhaps
Hali ibn el Abbas, a Persian, who died in A.D. 994; *Galien* is
Galen, the Greek physician of the second century; *Serapion* was
probably an Arabian physician of the eleventh or twelfth century; *Razis* is Rhazes of Baghdad, who lived during the ninth
and tenth centuries; *Avicen* and *Averrois* are Avicenna and
Averroës, the Arabian philosophers and physicians of the
eleventh and twelfth centuries respectively. The identity of
Damascien is uncertain. He may be either the elder Serapion or
one Yuhanna ibn Masawaih. Both lived during the ninth
century. *Constantyn* is Constantinus Afer, a monk of Carthage
who brought Arabian learning to Salerno in the eleventh century. *Bernard* is Bernard Gordon, a Scot, Professor of Medicine
at Montpellier about 1300; *Gatesden* is John of Gaddesden, of
Merton College, Oxford, who died in 1361; and *Gilbertyn* is
Gilbertus Anglicus, who lived in the latter part of the thirteenth century.

l. 441. esy of dispence. Sparing in his expenditure—*i.e.*, mean.

l. 442. that he wan in pestilence. Wealth which he had gained
during attacks of the plague. These were frequent in an age
which lacked real sanitation and was inclined to put illness down
to the will of God. The Black Death of 1348 was merely the
worst of a long series of such visitations, though they were
probably not all bubonic and rat-borne, as the Black Death
was.

l. 443. Another play on words. *Aurum potabile*, or drinkable gold,
was much used as a medicine. It was "gold held in a state of
minute sub-division in some volatile oil," according to the
Oxford English Dictionary.

l. 445. The West of England, and particularly Bath, was celebrated
in the fourteenth century, and for long afterwards, for its cloth.
Ypres and Ghent (l. 448) were great centres of the cloth trade.

l. 446. and that was scathe. "And that was a pity."

l. 450. offring. The offering was the collection in church. The
congregation went up in order to the priest, and the Wife of

Bath always insisted upon leading the file of women, as the most important person there.

l. 454. There may be some exaggeration here, but medieval head-dresses were often of great size and weight.

l. 460. The priest married the couple at the church-porch, and afterwards they entered the church and took part in the service of the Mass at the high altar.

l. 465–466. Boloigne. Boulogne, where there was (and still is) a celebrated image of the Virgin Mary.

Galice. Galicia, where at Compostella there was the shrine of St James.

Coloigne. Cologne, which contained the bodies of the three Kings, Gaspar, Melchior, and Balthazar, who visited the Manger at Bethlehem.

l. 468. Gat-tothed. With teeth set wide apart, a sign of good-luck, or, possibly, of an amorous disposition.

l. 475. remedyes. An allusion to Ovid's *Remedia Amoris*, a poem which explains how one may cure love. But there is no suggestion that the Wife knew anything of Ovid.

l. 476. the olde daunce. The old game; what was what. She knew all the arts of love.

l. 478. Persoun. A parish priest. These men were often of humble origin, little removed in social standing from their parishioners. Here, for instance, the Parson is the brother of the Plowman. He was poor because (as Manly suggests) the larger tithes were probably retained by some monastery or patron. In cases where the living was owned by a monastery or other patron the work of the parish was often performed by a 'vicarius,' for a stipend which represented only a small part of the value of the living. But this parson is presumably a rector, not a 'vicar.'

l. 486. to cursen. Failure to pay tithes was punishable in the last resort by excommunication, the most powerful weapon in the Church's armoury. But the Parson himself could not proceed to such lengths; that was a matter for the Bishop. The most he could do would be to refuse the sacraments to the offender, and report the offence.

l. 498. See St Matthew v, 19: "Whosoever therefore shall break one of these least commandments, and shall teach men so, he shall be called the least in the kingdom of heaven: but whosoever shall do and teach them, the same shall be called great in the kingdom of heaven."

l. 503. if a preest take keep. If a priest will but remember it.

l. 507. to hyre. It was a common practice for priests to hire substitutes to look after the parish while they themselves went to London and found easier, and more lucrative, employment as chantry-priests. Chantries were small chapels, containing the tombs of their founders, set apart in cathedrals and churches, and served by a priest whose business it was to say daily masses for the repose of the founder's soul. There were thirty-five such chapels in St Paul's in Chaucer's time, quite apart from those in the City churches.

l. 511. bretherhed. A priest could obtain employment as chaplain to one of the great guilds.

l. 526. spyced. "Spices" were fees (or bribes) paid to judges in advance to 'sweeten' their findings. The reference here is to an elastic conscience, a conscience open to a bargain.

l. 529. Plowman. Probably a small tenant farmer, or a free labourer working for wages: certainly not a serf.

l. 534. thogh him gamed or smerte. In pleasure or pain; in all circumstances. Robinson remarks that the Plowman, like his brother, is represented as an ideal Christian.

l. 541. a mere. A mare was regarded as a humble mount.

l. 548. the ram. A common prize at wrestling matches.

l. 550. nolde. Here in the sense of "could not," "could not have."

l. 560. goliardeys. A follower of the mythical Golias, head of the Order of the *Vagantes*, the wandering clerics. A buffoon, a teller of loose tales, and a singer of disreputable songs. See Helen Waddell, *The Wandering Scholars*, revised edition (London, 1932), pp. 183–187 and *passim*; F. J. E. Raby, *A History of Secular Latin Poetry in the Middle Ages*, Vol. II (Oxford, 1934), pp. 339–341.

l. 563. a thombe of gold. *Cf.* the proverb, "an honest miller has a golden thumb." That is, there are no honest millers. But Chaucer implies that this miller was honest enough, as millers go.

l. 567. Maunciple. Manciple, the official responsible for buying the provisions of a college, or—as here—one of the Inns of Court. In the Inner Temple, as Manly points out, he ranked below the cook. His inclusion among the pilgrims tends to support the theory that Chaucer studied law for some time.

l. 570. by taille. By tally, on credit. The price of the goods was scored on two strips of wood, and the purchaser and vendor each kept one. When the debt became due the creditor presented his tally as evidence. Examples of tallies can still be seen in the Museum of the Public Record Office.

l. 581. by his propre good. On his income.

l. 586. hir aller cappe. The caps of them all. 'To set some one's cap' was to make a fool of him. The sense here is "got the better of them."

l. 587. Reve. A steward or bailiff; more or less equivalent to the modern estate-agent. Manly believed that Chaucer had a particular reeve in mind, since he mentions the distant village of Baldeswell (modern Bawdswell) in Norfolk in connexion with him. This estate belonged to the earls of Pembroke, with whose family Chaucer had some legal business in 1378.

l. 589. Robinson says this was "a sign of his servile station"; but he was not a serf. It is true, however, that in earlier days the reeve was the serf who was elected annually to represent the interests of his fellows against the bailiff.

l. 602. No one could prove that he was in arrears.

l. 605. the deeth. The Plague, or possible death in general. *Cf.* the phrase, 'to hate some one like the plague.'

l. 618. rusty. He was no fighting man.

l. 623. Somnour. A summoner was an official whose duty it was to bring delinquents into the ecclesiastical courts, which dealt with marriage settlements, wills, tithes, other Church dues, and—most important of all, perhaps—moral offences.

l. 624. cherubinnes face. Red and flaming, like the faces of cherubim in illuminated MSS. and stained-glass windows. The cherubim were among the most important of the heavenly beings, and have nothing to do with the modern 'cherub,' a beautiful winged child, or child's head. Compare the difference between the medieval God of Love and the modern Cupid.

l. 625. sawcefleem. Pimpled. The Summoner was in fact suffering from alopecia, a form of leprosy, and he exhibits all the familiar marks of the disease, including scabby eyebrows and scanty (*piled*) beard.

l. 629–631. These lines describe the usual medieval remedies for this disease.

l. 643. Watte. Jays were taught to say "Wat" (or Walter) just as parrots are now taught to say "pretty Poll." But they understood what they were saying as much as the Summoner understood his Latin.

l. 644. But if anyone inquired further into his knowledge.

l. 646. *Questio quid iuris.* "What is the law on this point?" A phrase he had often heard in court.

l. 652. There can be no doubt that this line means that the Summoner himself had concubines in secret; the force of *eek* is perfectly clear. "To pluck a finch" had precisely this meaning, as Kittredge shows: *Modern Philology*, Vol. VII, pp. 476 and following. Skeat's suggestion that the phrase is equivalent to "plucking a pigeon," cheating an inexperienced person, cannot now be supported.

l. 653. a good felawe. Possibly in the sense of 'a boon companion'—certainly a rascal. *Cf.* l. 395.

l. 655. curs. Excommunication, which came under the archdeacon's control as head of the ecclesiastical court.

l. 658. "The only Hell known to the Archdeacon is being deprived of your money." The venality of the ecclesiastical courts was a constantly recurring complaint.

l. 662. *significavit*. The first word of a writ committing an excommunicated person to prison.

l. 663. In daunger. Under his control, at his mercy.

l. 664. yonge girles. Young people of both sexes.

l. 665. counseil. Secrets.
    was al hir reed. Was their sole adviser.

l. 666. gerland. Hoops of flowers, tied with ribbon and hung outside inns on the "ale-stake," or projecting pole. Sometimes the sign was a bush of ivy; hence the proverb, "Good wine needs no bush,"—*i.e.*, advertisement.
    The wreath of flowers (did he steal them from an inn?) and the shield made out of a round loaf show that the Summoner is drunk.

l. 669. Pardoner. Pardoners sold papal indulgences which commuted penances imposed for sins. The indulgences were written on pieces of parchment, with leaden seals of the papal office attached to them. The practice of selling these pardons rapidly became an abuse, and many so-called pardoners operated without authority, and were no better than swindlers. Chaucer's Pardoner is genuine enough—he was probably in minor orders—but even he, on his own showing, is a fraud.

l. 670. Rouncival. The subordinate house or hospital of Our Lady of Roncevaux (in Navarre) which stood near Charing Cross. There had been some scandal about the selling of pardons (ostensibly for the benefit of the house) by unauthorized persons in 1382 and 1387. Chaucer may have expected his readers to remember this.

l. 672. This is undoubtedly a refrain from a popular song of the day.

l. 673. "The Summoner supported him with a powerful bass part." The bourdon is a deep organ-stop, usually one of the sixteen-foot pipes.

l. 682. of the newe jet. In the latest fashion.

l. 685. A vernicle. A Veronica, a small image of the face of Christ. St Veronica is said to have lent Christ a handkerchief on His way to Calvary, and this received the imprint of His face. The Pardoner no doubt wore his vernicle as evidence that he had been to Rome, where the sacred handkerchief was preserved.

l. 692. From Berwick, in Northumberland, to Ware, in Hertford-shire—*i.e.*, from North to South.

l. 699. latoun. Latten, a mixture of copper and zinc much used in medieval times. It looked like modern brass, except that it was softer in colour. No doubt the Pardoner told his *apes* that it was gold.

l. 701. relikes. There was a vast trade in relics during the Middle Ages. Every religious house desired to possess as many as possible, for reasons which were sometimes of the highest, it is true, but were often merely concerned with their wonder-working (and therefore profitable) properties. The most brilliant attack on relics and relic-worship comes from Erasmus, in the *Colloquia*, where he describes a visit he paid to Becket's shrine in the company of his friend John Colet, Dean of St Paul's.

l. 702. A simple country parson.

l. 714. so merely. Manly-Rickert, Robinson; *the murierly*.

l. 726. "That you will not put it down to my lack of good manners."

l. 741. This remark of Plato Chaucer found in Boëthius, Book III, 12, or possibly in the *Roman de la Rose*, ll. 15,820–15,822.

l. 752. marshal. A master of ceremonies, who is required to be dignified, and tactful in the arrangement of guests in order of precedence.

l. 754. Chepe. Cheapside.

l. 760. A subtle touch. Genial as he was, the Host kept the best of his cheerfulness back until his guests had paid their bills.

l. 767. "I have just thought of something which will amuse you."

l. 803. gladly. Manly-Rickert, Robinson; *goodly*.

l. 823. our aller cok. The cock of us all; woke us all up.

l. 826. St Thomas-a-watering was a brook about a mile and a half out on the Canterbury road, a favourite place for watering horses.

l. 830. "If you are of the same mind this morning as you were last night."

l. 835. cut. Lots, by choosing straws from a bundle of different lengths.

l. 845. It was very proper that the most distinguished member of the party should tell the first tale. One cannot help feeling that the tactful Host had seen to it.

l. 858. In this manere. Manly-Rickert: *as ye may heere*.

The Pardoner's Tale (pp. 136–150)

We do not know precisely from what source Chaucer took this story, but it is certainly Oriental in origin and belongs to a collection known as the Jatakas, or birth-tales of Buddha. It is worth noting that Professor Carleton Brown, in his edition of the Tale, suggests that the story of the Wandering Jew may have given Chaucer the idea of the old man and his quest for Death. But the Prologue is entirely of his own invention.

The tale of the three *riotours* is one of the most masterly short stories in English, and Chaucer's power as a narrative poet is nowhere displayed to better advantage. Nothing is superfluous, the story moves swiftly to its appointed end, and it is perfectly balanced and rounded off. The interest and excitement are never allowed to flag, and the reader is left with that sense of warm satisfaction which always accompanies the contemplation of a piece of perfect craftsmanship. It may be noted that *The Pardoner's Tale* is probably in many respects a typical sermon, though no actual pardoner's sermon has been preserved, as far as we know. Miss Bowden remarks[1]:

> But not only is Chaucer's Pardoner accustomed to the pulpit. He is also a skilled demagogic orator who knows exactly the kind of sermons to preach that will thoroughly fascinate his audience, which in fact he later demonstrates in his own Tale; he knows how to read a lesson, too, or a series of lessons (a storie)—so that suspicious minds will be closed and purses opened—and how to capitalize on his soprano voice by singing the offertory the best of all, for the offertory precedes the sermon, and the tongue must be in smooth running order for that if silver is to be won. As Chaucer concludes, in a final burst of irony, our Canterbury-bound Pardoner is truly "a noble ecclesiaste"!

l. 1. Flaundres. Flanders, which in the fourteenth century had an unenviable reputation for drunkenness.

l. 15. tombesteres. Tumblers or acrobats, often to be seen in the

[1] *A Commentary on the General Prologue to the Canterbury Tales* (New York, 1949), p. 280.

Middle Ages, especially at great fairs, and even to-day by no means unknown on the music-hall stage. Here the reference is to dancing-girls.

l. 17. wafereres. Makers of wafer-cakes; confectioners. Skeat notes that in Elizabethan times they had a somewhat doubtful reputation.

l. 21. Probably Ephesians v, 18: "And be not drunk with wine, wherein is excess; but be filled with the Spirit."

l. 23. Loth. Lot. Genesis xix, 33–36.

l. 26. Herodes. Herod. See Matthew xiv, and Mark vi.
who-so wel the stories soghte. Whoever should examine the stores would find.
Skeat takes "the stories" to be the *Historia Evangelica* (and *Scholastica*) of Petrus Comestor, but possibly Chaucer means simply the Bible stories.

l. 30. Senek. Lucius Annæus Seneca (*c.* 4 B.C.–A.D. 65), the Stoic philosopher. The reference is to No. 83 of his Letters.

l. 37. A reference to the Fall of Man.

l. 39. boght us. Redeemed us.

l. 57. to-swinke. Manly's opinion is that this word does not exist; that no verb compounded with *to–* is used intransitively.

l. 60. I Corinthians vi, 13: "Meats for the belly, and the belly for meats: but God shall destroy both it and them."

l. 64. the whyte and rede. *I.e.*, wine.

l. 67. The apostel. St Paul. See Philippians iii, 18–19: "whose end is destruction, whose God is their belly, and whose glory is in their shame, who mind earthly things."

l. 77. An allusion to one of the most famous controversies of the Middle Ages, that between the Realists and the Nominalists. The former maintained that everything possesses an essential quality or substance which is independent of its outward appearance, the "accident" of Chaucer's phrase. Form, smell, taste, and colour are "accidents," and can be changed without affecting the real nature of a substance.

The application of all this is that cooks can often conceal the true nature of their ingredients by what they do with them. Medieval people were very fond of 'messes,' highly spiced and containing a mixture of many things.

l. 92. Sampsoun, Sampsoun. An excellent imitation of a drunken man's snore.

l. 93. For Samson, see Judges xiii–xvi.

l. 101. Lepe was in Spain, not far from Cadiz. We do not know exactly what sort of wine it was: possibly one similar to the 'sack' so beloved of the Elizabethans, a kind of sherry.

ll. 103–104. The joke here seems to be that Spanish wines were often sold as French, which were more expensive; and that the merchant often produced several different vintages from the same cask.

l. 109. La Rochelle and Bordeaux.

l. 117. Attila. King of the Huns, who died in 453.

l. 122. Lamuel. King Lemuel. See Proverbs xxxi, 4. "It is not for Kings, O Lemuel, it is not for kings to drink wine; nor for princes strong drink."

l. 141. Stilbon. Properly Chilon, a Spartan magistrate who was sent as ambassador to the Corinthians in the sixth century B.C.

l. 160. Parthes. The Parthians.

l. 172. See Matthew v, 34. "But I say unto you, Swear not at all. . . "

l. 173. See Jeremiah iv, 2. "And thou shalt swear, The Lord liveth, in truth, in judgment, and in righteousness; and the nations shall bless themselves in him, and in him shall they glory."

l. 189. The nails of the hands, not of the Cross. This is the sort of casual oath one might expect from a drunkard.

l. 190. Hayles. The Abbey of Hailes, in Gloucestershire, where a portion of the blood of Christ was preserved. It had been given to the Abbey in the thirteenth century by Richard, King of the Romans and brother of Henry III.

l. 191. An allusion to Hazard, described in the *Oxford English Dictionary* as "a game at dice in which the chances are complicated by a number of arbitrary rules." "It exists to-day practically unchanged under the name Craps"—Manly.
cink and treye. Cinq et trois, five and three.

l. 202. A hand-bell was rung by the sexton walking before the corpse.

l. 211. to-night. Last night.

l. 217. Possibly an allusion to the Black Death.

l. 236. The custom of plighting sworn brotherhood was taken very seriously: it had almost legal binding force. It was sometimes resorted to before going on a long journey overseas.

l. 247. they to-rente. Manly-Rickert, Robinson; *al torente*.

l. 272. cheste. A box containing all his worldly possessions.

l. 274. Heyre clout. *I.e.*, for burial.

ll. 281–282. Leviticus xxi, 32 is alluded to here. "Thou shalt rise up before the hoary head, and honour the face of the old man, and fear thy God: I am the Lord."

l. 308. florins. The florin was a gold coin worth 6s. 8d.

l. 328. Thieves could be (and were) hanged for what we should now consider trifling offences; a state of affairs which lasted until the beginning of the nineteenth century.

l. 331. cut. See the note to l. 835 of the *Prologue*.

l. 396. destroyed. Worried, harassed.

l. 427. Avicen. Avicenna, the great Arabian physician. His best-known work was *The Book of the Canon of Medicine*. It is divided into books, and each book is divided into 'fens' or sections, which are further divided into tractates.

l. 433. ful of cursednesse. Manly-Rickert, Robinson; *of alle cursed-nesse*.

l. 445. sterlinges. Silver pennies. Some of the Norman pennies had a small star (sterling) on one side.

l. 446. broches. Brooches, rings, and plate were often used instead of currency during the Middle Ages.

l. 466. tounes ende. Manly-Rickert, Robinson; *myles ende*.

l. 483. grote. Groat, a silver coin worth four silver pennies.

The Parson's Tale (pp. 150–153)

Sequitur de Accidia

No direct source for this tale has been found, but it seems clear that a good deal of it derives from the *Summa seu Tractatus de Viciis* of Gulielmus Peraldus (*c.* 1260) and the *Summa Casuum Pœnitentiæ* of St Raymond of Pennaforte (*c.* 1240). But precisely how and in what form these works reached Chaucer is not known.

The Parson's Tale is a sermon on the subject of penitence, into which has been inserted a long digression on the subject of the Seven Deadly Sins, that staple theme of the medieval preacher. But it has nothing of Langland's vivid and powerful presentation of them as living persons, which is one of the finest passages in the whole of medieval literature.

Accidie is a sin difficult to define. It is sloth, but more than mere physical laziness. It is complete mental and spiritual inertia, often caused by consciousness of sin, which robs a man of all joy in life and makes it impossible for him either to think or act. To its victims everything is utterly without worth or savour. Ultimately it leads to despair, the sin against the Holy Ghost. It is perhaps significant that it was originally thought of as the acute boredom which attacked monks and nuns, or recluses committed to perpetual seclusion. See G. G. Coulton, *Five Centuries of Religion* (Cambridge, 1923), Vol. I, pp. 97–98; 165–166.

l. 7. Augustin. From his treatise on Psalm iv.

l. 11. Salomon. Ecclesiastes ix, 10. "Whatsoever thy hand findeth to do, do it with thy might; for there is no work, nor device, nor knowledge, nor wisdom, in the grave, whither thou goest."

l. 14. the book. Jeremiah xlviii, 10. "Cursed be he that doeth the work of the Lord deceitfully, and cursed be he that keepeth back his sword from blood." The Vulgate has "fraudulenter" for "negligently."

l. 38. seint Johan. Revelation iii, 16. "So then because thou art lukewarm, and neither cold nor hot, I will spue thee out of my mouth."

l. 41. Salomon. Proverbs xviii, 9. "He also that is slothful in his work is brother to him that is a great waster." See also xx, 4; and xxi, 25.

l. 48. seint Bernard . . . seint Gregorie. These references have not yet been identified.

l. 64. Augustin. Skeat refers to his *De Natura et Gratia* and *Sermo XX*.

l. 92. Axe and have. Matthew vii, 7. "Ask, and it shall be given you; seek, and ye shall find; knock, and it shall be opened unto you." See also John xvi, 24.

l. 101. Salomon. Proverbs viii, 17. "I love them that love me; and those that seek me early shall find me."

l. 102. Necligence. Robinson compares the prologue of the "Second Nun's Tale," ll. 1–3.

> The ministre and the norice unto vices,
> Which that men clepe in Englissh ydelnesse,
> That porter of the gate is of delices. . . .

l. 107. the wyse man. Robinson refers to Ecclesiastes vii, 19 (Vulgate). "Bonum est te sustentare justum; sed et ab illo ne subtrahas manum tuam; quia qui timet Deum, nihil negligit."

HERE TAKETH THE MAKERE OF THIS BOOK HIS LEVE
(pp. 153–154)

l. 15. the nynetene Ladies. So Skeat. But most MSS. give the the number as twenty-five.

l. 18. The book of the Leoun. This was possibly a translation, now lost, of Machaut's *Dit dou Leon*.

BIBLIOGRAPHY

The following is a short list of books which will be found useful as an introduction to the study of Chaucer and the Middle Ages.

Editions

SKEAT, W. W.: *The Complete Works of Geoffrey Chaucer* (Oxford, 1894–95).

The Student's Chaucer (Oxford, 1895).

POLLARD, A. W., AND OTHERS: *The "Globe" Chaucer* (London, 1898).

MANLY, J. M.: *Canterbury Tales* (New York, 1928).

ROBINSON, F. N.: *The Poetical Works of Chaucer* (Harvard, 1933).

Critical Works

LOWELL, J. R.: *My Study Windows* (Boston, 1871).

LOUNSBURY, T. R.: *Studies in Chaucer* (New York, 3 vols., 1892).

LEGOUIS, É.: *Geoffrey Chaucer* (Paris, 1910; London, 1913).

BRUSENDORFF, A.: *The Chaucer Tradition* (Oxford, 1925).

COWLING, G. H.: *Chaucer* (London, 1927).

FRENCH, R. D.: *A Chaucer Handbook* (New York, 1927).

MANLY, J. M.: *Some New Light on Chaucer* (New York, 1927).

KITTREDGE, G. L.: *Chaucer and his Poetry* (Harvard, 1933).

LOWES, J. L.: *Geoffrey Chaucer* (Oxford, 1934).

GOFFIN, R. C.: *Troilus and Criseyde* (Oxford, 1935).

SHELLEY, P. VAN DYKE: *The Living Chaucer* (Pennsylvania, 1940).

BRYAN AND DEMPSTER: *Sources and Analogues of Chaucer's Canterbury Tales* (Chicago, 1941).

CHESTERTON, G. K.: *Chaucer* (London, 1948).

PATCH, H. R.: *On Re-reading Chaucer* (Harvard, 1948).

BOWDEN, MURIEL: *A Commentary on the General Prologue of the Canterbury Tales* (New York, 1949).

COGHILL, NEVILL: *The Poet Chaucer* (London, 1949).

SPEIRS, JOHN: *Chaucer the Maker* (London, 1951).

Studies of Chaucer's Period

TRAILL, H. D.: *Social England* (revised edition, 6 vols., London, 1901–4).

COULTON, G. G.: *Chaucer and his England* (London, 1908).

KER, W. P.: *English Literature: Mediæval* (London, 1912).

HADOW, G.: *Chaucer and his Times* (London, 1914).

DAVIES, H. W. C. (editor): *Mediæval England* (Oxford, 1924).

JUSSERAND, J. J.: *Wayfaring Life in the Middle Ages* (English translation: London, 1925).

SALZMAN, L. F.: *English Life in the Middle Ages* (Oxford, 1926).

COULTON, G. G.: *The Mediæval Scene* (Cambridge, 1930).

BENNETT, H. S.: *Life on the English Manor* (Cambridge, 1937).

COULTON, G. G.: *Mediæval Panorama* (Cambridge, 1938).

TREVELYAN, G. M.: *English Social History* (London, 1944).

BENNETT, H. S.: *Chaucer and the Fifteenth Century* (Oxford, 1947).

RICKERT, E.: *Chaucer's World* (Oxford, 1949).

aboghte, pret. sing., paid for, bought dearly; from 'abye.'

aboven, above.

a-breyde, to awake.

abye, to pay for.

accidie, sloth. See the introduction to the Parson's Tale p. 191.

achat, purchase, buying.

achatours, purchasers, caterers.

acloyeth, overburdens.

acordaunt, suitable.

acorde, to agree, allow.

adouringe, adoration.

adrad, p.p., afraid.

adversarie, hostile.

a-fere, on fire.

a-ferd, p.p., afraid.

afounde, to perish.

affray, fright.

affraye, to frighten.

affyle, to file, make smooth.

agaste, pret. sing., frightened; from 'agaste.'

ageyn, against.

a-go, p.p., gone; from 'agon.'

a-gref, amiss.

aguiler, needle-case.

al, awl; *to sporne ageyn an al* (*Truth*, l.11), to kick against the pricks.

al, (conj.) although.

Alcipyades, Alcibiades.

alderbest, best of all.

alderlevest, dearest of all.

aldermost, most of all.

alderwysest, wisest of all.

alestake, ale-stake, a pole supporting a sign or bush outside an inn.

aleyes, alleys, walks.

algate, in any case, nevertheless.

Alisaundre, Alexander the Great; Alexandria.
aller, of all; gen. plural of 'al.'
almesse, alms.
also, as.
amblere, an ambling horse.
amis, seyde, gave an unwelcome answer.
amorwe, in the morning.
anlas, a short dagger.
annexed, p.p., attached; from 'annexe.'
anoint, p.p., anointed; from 'anointe.'
anon, immediately.
anoy, trouble, vexation.
anoye, to annoy, vex, harm.
apaye, to satisfy; *evel apayd*, ill-pleased.
ape, dupe.
apese, to appease, pacify.
apparaunte, clear, apparent.
appreved, p.p., proved, confirmed; from 'appreve.'
apyked, p.p., trimmed, adorned; from 'apyke.'
arede, to divine, interpret.
areste, to stop.
aretten, to impute.
armes, feats of arms.
armonye, harmony.
a-roume, at large, in an open space.
array, dress.
arrerage, arrears.
artow, art thou.
aryve, landing, disembarkation of troops.
as, as if.
ascaunces, as if to say.
aspye, spy.
assay, trial.
assaye, to try, make trial of, test.
assege, siege.
assent, agreement, opinion.
assente, to agree to.
assoilen, to absolve, pardon; *assoiling*, pardon.

assure, to comfort, give assurance to.
astoned, p.p., confounded, overcome; from 'astonie.'
astonie, to astonish, confound.
astored, stored, provided.
astronomye, astrology.
asweved, p.p., dazed, put to sleep; from 'asweve.'
a-swown, in a swoon.
attempre, temperate, mild.
a-two, in two.
auctoritee, authority.
auctour, author.
aungellyke, like an angel.
avaunce, to advance, promote, aid, be profitable.
avaunt, boast.
avauntour, boaster.
aventure, chance, luck, fortune; happening.
avys, advice, counsel.
avyse, to consider, take heed.
avysement, consideration.
aweye, done with, over.
awhape, to amaze, confound.
axen, to ask.
ay, always, ever.
ayeins, ayen, against, in.

Babiloyne, Babylon.
bachelere, an aspirant to knighthood.
bake mete, baked meats; meat-pies.
balled, bald.
bane, death.
baren, pret. plural, bore.
barbe, barb, part of a woman's headdress; a piece of plaited linen reaching from the chin to the waist.
barge, ship.
barm-clooth, apron.
barres, bars, bands, small pieces of metal.
baudes, bawds.
baudrik, baldric, belt worn over the shoulder.

bawme, balm.

bayten, to bask, rest.

beet, pret. sing., adjoined; from 'bete.'

beforn, before.

beggestere, beggar (properly a female beggar).

behette, pret. sing., promised; from 'bihote.'

benched, provided with benches.

benigne, benign, kind, gracious.

bent, p.p., arched; from 'bende.'

be-set, wel, proper, right.

beste, beast.

bet, better; *go bet*, go as quickly as possible.

betid, p.p. happened; from 'bityde.'

betraysed, p.p., betrayed; from 'bitraise.'

bever, beaver.

beye, to buy, pay for.

bicched, cursed.

bidde, to ask, pray.

bifore, al, in front of other people; leading the way.

biforn, before.

bihove, to suit.

bileve, belief, faith.

bile, bill, beak.

binime, to take away.

binne, bin, chest.

biseken, to beseech, pray.

bisette, pret. sing., employed; from 'bisette.'

bisily, busily, diligently, attentively.

bisinesse, business, diligence, industry.

bismotered, p.p., stained.

bisy, busy, industrious; *bisily*, eagerly, attentively.

bisyde, beside, near.

bit, pres. sing., bids; from 'bidde.'

bitraise, to betray; *bitrasshed*, betrayed.

bityde, to betide, happen.

bi-wryen, to reveal, disclose, betray.

blankmanger, creamed fowl or other meat stewed with eggs, rice, almonds, and sugar (Robinson).

blende, to blind, deceive.

blent, pres. sing., blinds; from 'blende.'

blythe, happy, glad.

blyve, quickly, soon.

boke, book.

bokeler, buckler; a small round shield.

bole, bull.

bond, pret. sing., bound; from 'binde.'

bone, boon, prayer, request.

boon, bone, ivory; dice.

boras, borax.

bord, board, table; *he had the bord bigonne*, he had sat at the head of the table.

borwe, pledge.

bote, remedy.

boteler, butler.

botes, boots.

botme, bottom.

bourde, to jest.

bracer, bracer, a guard for the arm in archery.

bragot, bragget, a drink made of honey and ale.

braste, pret. sing., burst; from 'breste.'

breech, breeches.

breed, bread.

brekke, break, flaw, defect.

brende, pret. sing., burned; from 'brenne.'

brenne, to burn.

breste, to break, burst.

bretful, brimful.

bretherhed, brotherhood, guild.

brid, bird.

brighte, brightness.

broche, brooch.

brode, broadly, plainly.

brood, broad.

brotelnesse, frailty, insecurity.

brouke, to enjoy, use.

brydel, bridle.

bulle, Papal Bull, document.
burdoun, bass accompaniment, ground melody.
burgeys, burgess, citizen.
busk, bush.
but, but-if, except, unless.
buxomnesse, submission.

caas, cas, chance, circumstance; case (of law).
caityf, wretch.
can, knew, had; from 'conne.'
canel-boon, collar-bone.
canon, canon, rule.
capoun, capon.
cappe, cap; *sette hir aller cappe*, made fools of them.
carf, pret. sing., carved, cut; from 'kerve.'
carie, to carry, convey; in Prol., l.130, to carry (a piece of meat)
   from the centre dish to her plate.
carl, man, fellow, rustic.
carole, carol, a dance and song combined.
carpe, to talk.
Cartage, Carthage.
cas, case, chance; *up-on cas*, by chance.
caste, to cast—*e.g.*, a horoscope; contrive, plan.
catel, property, possessions, 'chattels.'
ceint, girdle, belt.
celle, cell, religious house; *keeper of the celle*, prior.
certein, adj., sure, true; adv., certainly, indeed.
certes, certainly.
ceruce, white lead.
chapman, merchant.
charge, burden, responsibility.
chargeaunt, burdensome.
charitable, kind.
charitee, charity.
chaunterie, chantry, an endowment for the payment of a priest to
   sing requiem masses for the founder's soul.
chelaundre, a species of lark.
Chepe, Cheapside.

cheeste, pres. sing., chooses; from 'chese.'

chere, face, appearance; behaviour.

cherubinnes, cherub's.

chese, to choose.

chevisaunce, borrowing, lending, dealing.

chicknes, chickens.

chiteringe, chattering, chirping.

chivachye, a military expedition on horseback.

cink, cinque, five.

Cipioun, Scipio Africanus Minor.

circumscryve, to enclose, comprehend.

clause, sentence; *in a clause*, briefly.

clene, clean, pure, entirely; elegant, elegantly.

clennesse, cleanness, purity.

clepen, to call.

clere, clear, bright, pure.

clerk, cleric, scholar.

clomben, p.p., climbed; from 'climben.'

clobbed, clubbed, club-shaped.

cloisterer, a resident in a cloister, monk; *cloisterlees*: outside the cloister.

close, pret. sing., include.

clout, piece of cloth; rag.

cod, bag, stomach.

cofre, coffer, chest.

coke, cook.

colde, to chill.

colere, choler, anger, irascibility.

colerik, choleric, hot-tempered.

collateral, subordinate.

colour, colour, appearance; in rhetoric, figures of speech, fine phrases.

colpons, shreds, strips.

commeveth, pres. sing., moves, instigates, induces; from 'commeve.'

compeer, comrade, close friend.

composicioun, agreement.

condicioun, condition, state, character.

confiture, mixture, preserve.
conning, knowledge, skill.
conscience, feelings, sympathy.
conseil, council, counsel, advice, secret.
contree, area, region.
convers, converse, reverse.
cop, top.
cope, cope, cape, cloak.
coppe, cup.
corage, heart, mind, disposition.
corn, a grain.
corone, coroune, crown, garland.
cors, corpse.
corve, p.p., cut; from 'kerve.'
costeying, pres. part., coasting, walking along; from 'costeye.'
coude, pret. sing., knew; from 'conne.'
counseil, counsel, secrets.
countenaunce, appearance, looks.
countour, auditor, arithmetician.
courtepy, short upper coat.
couthe, pret. sing., could; *as he couthe,* as well as he could.
couthe, known.
covenable, proper, suitable.
covenaunt, agreement.
coverchief, kerchief worn on the head.
covetyse, covetousness.
covyne, deceitfulness.
coy, quiet, shy, modest.
craft, skill or trade.
creant, seith; acknowledges defeat.
croked, crooked; crooked things.
crokke, earthenware pot.
crop, top, new twig.
croys, cross.
crulle, curly.
cryke, creek.
cunning, skill, ability.
curat, parish priest.

cure, cure, care; *I do no cure*, I care not.
curious, careful, diligent, skilful; delicately made, ornate.
cursen, curse, excommunicate.
cursing, excommunication.
curteys, courteous.
curteisye, courtesy, good-breeding.
cut, draweth, draw lots (imperative).

daliaunce, gossip, social conversation, toying, caressing.
dame, mother, wife.
dampne, to condemn.
dan, daun, contraction of *dominus*, lord, sir, master.
daswed, p.p., dazed, confused; from 'daswen.'
daunce, dance.
daunger, disdain, power, control.
daungerous, imperious, disdainful.
daunten, to daunt, terrify, subdue, tame.
daweth, pres. sing., dawns, from 'dawe.'
dede, deed, dead; *dede slepe*, heavy sleep.
deedly, deedlich, deadly, mortally.
deef, deaf.
dees, dice.
dees, dais.
deeth, death, the plague.
defaute, fault, defect.
defende, to defend, forbid.
defet, p.p., exhausted.
degree, rank.
delitous, delightful.
deliver, agile, quick.
delve, to dig.
deme, to judge, decide.
departe, to part, separate.
desolaat, holden, shunned.
despitous, spiteful, scornful.
destroyed, harassed, disturbed.
devys, at his, according to his wishes.
deye, to die.

deyntee, pleasure.

deyntee, adj., rare, fine.

deys, dais.

diffyne, to define.

digneliche, disdainfully, scornfully, perhaps formally.

digne, worthy, honourable; proud, haughty.

dint, stroke.

dischevele, with hair loose.

discryve, to describe.

disese, discomfort, misery, sorrow.

disobeysaunt, disobedient.

dispence, expenditure.

dispitously, angrily, spitefully.

displesant, displeasing.

disport, sport, amusement: *of greet disport*, very entertaining.

disteyne, to stain, bedim.

distreyne, to constrain.

ditee, ditty, song.

doke, duck.

dokked, docked, cut short.

domb, dumb.

done, to, to be done.

donne, dun, dusky.

doom, dome, judgment.

doseyn, dozen.

doumb, dumb.

doutances, perplexities.

douten, to fear.

drede, dread, doubt; *it is no drede*, there is no doubt; certainly.

dredeles, certainly, undoubtedly.

dredful, terrible, fearful, timid.

dreint, pret. sing., drowned; from 'drenchen.'

dresse, to direct, prepare, make ready.

dreye, dry.

drogges, drugs.

droghte, drought.

dronkelewe, drunk, addicted to drink.

drow, pret, sing., drew, inclined; from 'drawe.'

drye, to endure, suffer.
dulle, to feel or make dull, to become stupefied, bored.
dwelle, to remain, stay.
dyke, to dig ditches.
dytees, ditties, songs.

Ecclesiaste, divine, minister.
Ector, Hector.
eek, eke, also.
eem, uncle.
effect, deed, reality; *in effect*, in fact.
eft, again, later, another time.
eleccioun, choice.
Eleyne, Helen of Troy.
elles, else, otherwise.
elvish, elvish, not of this world.
embrouded, p.p., embroidered.
emperice, empress.
empryse, enterprise, undertaking.
enbrace, to embrace.
enclyne, to bow (to), incline before.
encrees, increase.
endyte, to write, compare.
enlumined, illumined.
ensample, example.
entende, to attend, give attention to.
ententif, attentive.
ententifly, attentively.
entree, entry, entrance.
entremeten (him), meddle with; from 'entremette.'
entryketh, ensnares.
entune, to intone.
envoluped, p.p., enveloped.
envye, envy, desire; *to envye*, in rivalry.
envyned, provided or stocked with wine.
er, before.
erchedeken, archdeacon.
Ercules, Hercules.

erme, to feel sad, grieve.
erratik, wandering.
erst, first.
eschaunge, exchange.
ese, to ease, relieve.
espye, spy.
estat, state, condition, rank.
estatlich, stately, dignified.
esy, pleasant, gentle; moderate.
evene, even, equal, moderate, exactly.
everich, everichoon, every one.
everydeel, every bit.
ever-mo, for ever, always, continually.
excusacioun, excuse.
expresly, expressly, exactly, definitely.

facound, eloquent.
facounde, eloquence, fluency.
facultee, capacity, power, official position.
fair, fine, fair, good; *a fair,* a good one.
faire, fairly; *faire mot she falle,* may she have good fortune.
falding, coarse cloth.
falsen, to falsify, deceive, betray.
famulier, familiar, intimate.
fantasye, fancy, imagination.
farsed, p.p., filled, stuffed; from 'farce.'
faste, closely, near.
faunen, to fawn (on)
feer, fear.
feend, fiend, devil.
felawe, companion, comrade; sometimes used contemptuously.
felde, field.
felen, to feel, experience, perceive.
fen, chapter or subdivision.
fendes, fiends, devils.
fer, far.
ferd, afeared, frightened.
ferde, pret. sing., fared; from 'faren.'

fere, companion.

ferne, distant.

ferre, farther: *ferrest,* farthest.

ferthing, farthing, small portion.

fest, fist.

feste, feast, festival, merriment.

festne, to fasten.

fet, pret. sing., fetched; from 'fecchen.'

fetys, well-made, neat.

fetisly, elegantly.

fey, faith.

feynest, most gladly.

figure, figure, shape; figure of speech.

fil, pret. sing., fell; from 'fallen.'

filet, fillet, headband.

finder, discoverer.

fithele, an early stringed instrument, ancestor of the violin.

Flaundrish, Flemish.

flemen, to banish.

flete, to float.

flex, flax.

florouns, florets, petals.

flour-de-lys, fleur-de-lis, lily.

floytinge, playing on the flute.

folye, folly.

fond, pret. sing., found; from 'finde.'

fool, adj., foolish.

foon, foes.

foot-mantel, foot-cloth, protection for the skirt.

forbereth, imperative plural, forgive; from 'forbere.'

forby, by, past.

for-dronke, extremely drunk.

for-leten, to abandon, forsake, lose.

forme, form, formality.

formel, mate (used of birds), companion.

forneys, furnace.

for-pyned, p.p., wasted away.

fors, force; *no fors,* no matter.

forshapen, p.p., metamorphosed, transformed.
forsleweth, pres. sing., wastes idly.
forsluggeth, pres. sing., spoils.
forster, forester, game-keeper.
forsweringe, perjury.
fortheren, to further, advance.
for-thy, therefore.
fortunen, to happen, befall, render fortunate, interpret favourably.
for-waked, p.p., tired out by watching.
forward, agreement.
forweped, exhausted by weeping.
for-why, wherefore, why, because.
forwrapped, p.p., wrapped up.
foryeve, to forgive.
fother, load, great quantity.
foudre, thunderbolt.
foul, bird.
fouler, fowler.
frankeleyn, franklin, freeholder.
fraternitee, brotherhood, guild.
free, liberal, generous-minded.
freedom, liberality, generous conduct.
fret, ornament.
fro, from.
fruytesteres, fruit-sellers.
ful, full, satiated.
fulle, atte, completely.
fumositee, fumes arising from the stomach, caused by drink.
furtheringes, help.
fustian, fustian, thick cotton cloth.
fyn, end, result.

Galauntyne, sauce.
galingale, sweet cyperus, a spice.
game, sport, entertainment.
gamed, pret. sing. impers., it pleased.
gan, pret. sing., began; from 'ginne.'
gat-toothed, with teeth set wide apart.

gauded, p.p., furnished with 'gauds' or beads.
Gaunt, Ghent.
gay, finely dressed, joyous.
gent, refined, exquisite.
gentil, courteous, well-bred.
gentilly, courteously.
gere, equipment, armour.
gerland, garland, wreath.
gerner, granary.
gesse, to suppose, imagine.
geste, tale, romance, story.
gilt, guilt, offence.
ginglen, to jingle.
ginneth, pres. sing., begins; from 'ginne.'
gipoun, short doublet or cassock.
gipser, pouch, purse.
girles, young people, of both sexes.
giterne, guitar, cittern.
gledy, glowing, burning.
glee, music, entertainment.
glose, comment, commentary, explanation.
glotoun, glutton.
gobet, piece, morsel.
goddes, gods.
golee, gabble.
golet, gullet, throat.
goliardeys, buffoon, jester, scurrilous talker.
gomme, gum.
gon, to go, proceed.
good, property, goods.
goodly, patiently, kindly.
goot, goat.
gore, gusset of a garment, a triangular piece let in to strengthen or enlarge it.
gost, spirit.
grace, favour, mercy; *with sory grace,* "bad luck to you," "curse you."
grayn, dye.

O

gree, favour, good part, goodwill; *in gree*, favourably.
grette, pret. sing., greeted; from 'grete.'
gretter, greater.
gretteste, greatest.
greves, boughs, sprays.
grille, horrible.
grisly, horrible, terrible.
grope, to test, examine.
grote, groat.
ground, ground, foundation; texture.
grys, grey fur.
guerdoning, reward.
gunne, pret. plural, began; from 'ginne.'
gye, to guide.
gyse, guise, manner.

habounde, to abound.
habergeoun, coat of mail.
habit, dress.
half, side, part; *on my halfe*, from me.
hals, neck, throat.
halwes, saints, shrines.
han, pres. plural, have; from 'have.'
hap, chance, luck, good fortune.
happe, to happen, befall.
hardily, boldly, certainly, scarcely.
hardy, bold.
harlot, low fellow, rascal.
harlotrye, ribaldry, wickedness.
harneised, p.p., equipped, mounted.
harre, hinge.
hasard, hazard, a game of dice; gaming.
hasardrye, gaming.
hastow, hast thou.
haunt, abode; practice, skill.
haunteden, pret. pl., practised; from 'haunten.'
hawe, yard, enclosure.
hay, hedge.

hed, p.p., hidden; from 'hyde.'

heed, head.

heer, hair.

heighe and lowe, in, in all respects.

helpe, to help, cure.

hem, them.

henne, hence.

hente, to catch, seize, get.

herber, garden, arbour.

herberwe, harbour, lodging, shelter, inn.

herde, herd, keeper of cattle.

here, to hear.

hermyte, hermit.

Herodes, Herod.

hertely, heartily, truly.

heryinge, praising.

heste, command, promise; *hestes*, the Commandments.

hete, pret. sing., was called; from 'hote.'

hethenesse, heathen lands.

heve, to heave, lift.

heved, head.

hevenish, heavenly.

heyre (adj. and subst.) hair.

heyre, (subst.) heir.

heysugge, hedge-sparrow.

hider, hither.

highte, pret. sing., was called, named; from 'hote.'

hindreste, hindmost, last.

hir, her, their.

hit, it.

holde, to keep, preserve.

holde, p.p., bound, obliged; from 'holde.'

holly, hoolly, wholly.

holpe, holpen, p.p., helped; from 'helpe.'

holt, plantation, wood.

holwe, hollow, thin.

hond, hand.

honest, honourable, worthy, creditable.

honge, to hang; *doon us honge,* have us hanged.
hoor, white-haired.
hoot, hot.
hord, avarice.
hors, horse; also plural.
hostiler, innkeeper.
houres, hours, for astrological use.
humblesse, humility.
hust, hushed, silent.
hye, (adv.) high, loudly.
hye, (subst.) haste.
hye, (verb) to hasten.
hyer, higher, upper.
hyne, hind, servant.
hyre, hire, reward.

ilke, same, very.
inde, indigo, dark blue; India.
infect, invalid, of no effect, dimmed.
inspired, p.p., quickened.
Isoude, Isolde, Iseult.

janglere, story-teller, jester.
jape, jest, trick.
jet, fashion; *the newe jet,* the latest style.
jolif, joyful, merry.
jolitee, sport, amusement.
Jonathas, Jonathan.
juste, to joust, tourney.
justyse, justice, administration of justice.

kembe, to comb.
kepe (subst.), heed.
kepe (verb), keep, preserve, take care of, protect.
kid, p.p., made known; from 'kythen.'
kinde, nature, race, stock.
knarre, thick-set fellow.
knave, boy, servant-lad.

knet, joined; from 'knitte.'
knobbes, large pimples.

laas, lace, cord.
lachesse, laziness.
Lacidomie, Lacedæmon, Sparta.
lad, p.p., led; from 'lede.'
lafte, pret. sing., left; from 'leve.'
lakke, lack, want, defect.
lakken, to find fault with.
large, large, liberal, generous.
large, (adv.) freely.
las, lace, snare.
lasse, less.
late, lately, recently.
latoun, latten, a mixture of copper and zinc.
lay, lay, song.
layser, leyser, leisure.
lazar, leper.
leche, physician.
leed, lead (metal); cauldron (Prol., l. 202).
leef, dear, precious; desirous, anxious (Pardoner's Tale, l. 298).
lees, untrue.
leet, pret. sing., left; from 'lete.'
lege, to lay; from 'leye.'
lendes, loins.
lene, (adj.) lean, thin, weak.
lene, to lend, give.
lere, to teach, learn.
lese, to lose.
lesing, lie, falsehood.
lesse, less, thinner.
lest, pleasure, delight.
lest, pres. sing. impers., it pleases; *whyl hem leste,* as long as it pleased them.
leste, least.
let, pres. sing., leads; from 'lede.'
lete, to let, leave, give up.

leting, pres. part., leaving; from 'lete.'

lette, to hinder, stop.

letuarie, electuary, remedy.

leve, dear.

leve, to believe.

lever, rather; *me were lever*, I had rather.

lewed, ignorant, ill-bred.

lewednes, ignorance; ill-breeding.

leyser, leisure.

licentiat, one licensed by the Pope to hear confessions.

licour, moisture, liquor, juice.

light, joyous, light-hearted, easy.

lightly, lightly, quickly, easily.

likerous, lecherous.

limitour, a friar licensed to beg for alms within a certain limit.

lipsed, pret. sing., lisped.

lisse, comfort, relief.

lissen, to alleviate.

list, pres. sing. impers., it pleases.

litarge, litharge, ointment prepared from protoxide of lead.

livestow, livest thou.

lodemenage, pilotage.

loke, look, appearance.

lond, land; *up-on lond*, in the country.

longeth, pres. pl., belong; from 'longe.'

loos, loose, free.

looth, loath, unwilling.

lordinges, sirs.

lore, learning, knowledge.

lore, p.p., lost; from 'lese.'

loth, loath, displeasing.

lother, more hateful.

lough, pret. sing., laughed; from 'laughe.'

love-dayes, days for settling disputes by arbitration.

lovyere, lover.

lowly, humble.

luce, luce, pike.

lust, desire, pleasure, delight.

lustily, gaily, merrily.
lusty, pleasant, happy, joyous.
luxurie, lechery.
lyflode, means of living, livelihood.
lyke, to please.
lykne, to compare, liken.
lyte, little.

maad, p.p., made; from 'make.'
Macedoyne, Macedonia.
Macrobes, Macrobius.
maister, master, one in authority.
maistrye, mastery, control, skill; *a fair for the maistrye,* an extremely fine one.
make, mate.
make, to compose, write.
male, bag, wallet.
manere, manner, way; *maneres,* kinds.
mantel, mantle, cloak.
mark, a piece of money valued at 13*s.* 4*d.*
mary, marrow, pith.
mary-bones, marrow-bones.
mat, dejected, exhausted.
materes, matters, subjects, materials.
me, by, on my own account.
mede, mead, meadow.
medewe, meadow.
medlee, of a mixed colour.
meed, mede, reward.
meeth, mead, a drink made of fermented honey and water.
mene, mean, middle course.
mere, mare.
merlioun, merlin, small hawk.
meschief, misfortune.
messagere, messenger.
mesurable, moderate.
mete, (adj.) equal.
mete, (subst.) meat, food; dinner.

mete, (verb) to dream.

mette, pret. sing., dreamed; from 'mete.'

mewe, mew, coop.

meynee, household, retinue.

might, over hir, beyond their capacity.

mirtheles, sad.

mirth, pleasure, something entertaining.

miscarie, to go amiss, come to harm.

mismetre, pres. sing. subj., scan wrongly.

mister, trade, occupation, office.

mo, more, greater, another.

moche, mochel, much.

moder, mother.

moiste, supple.

mone, moon.

moot, mote, pret. sing., must, shall.

more and lasse, great and small; every one.

mormal, sore, gangrene, ulcer.

mortreux, thick soups, stew.

morwe, morning, morrow.

morwe-song, morning-song.

morwe-tyde, morning-time, morning hour.

moste, most, greatest.

mot, pret. sing., must; from 'moot'; *to goode mote it turn,* may it turn to good.

mottelee, motley, parti-coloured cloth.

mountance, amount, quantity.

mowen, to be able; *mowe,* pret. sing., may.

muche, much; *muche and lyte,* high and low.

murye, merry.

nam, am not (ne am).

namely, especially.

namo, no more.

narwe, narrow, small.

nas, ne was, was not.

natheles, nevertheless.

nay, nay, no; *it is no nay,* there is no denying it.

ne, not.

neet, neat, cattle.

nere, nearer.

nere; ne were; second person, pret. sing., wast not; pret. plural, were not.

nevene, to name.

never-a-del, never a bit, not at all.

nighter-tale, night-time.

nil, pres. sing., will not.

nis, is not (ne is).

noble, a gold coin worth 6*s.* 8*d.*

nones, for the; for the occasion, then.

Noon, none, no one.

noot, first person, pret. sing., know not (ne wot).

norice, nurse.

norissing, nutriment, sustenance, nourishment.

nose-thirles, nostrils.

note, note, tune.

not-heed, head with hair cut short.

nother, neither.

nouthe, now; *as nouthe,* just now.

noyous, troublesome.

nyce, foolish, scrupulous.

nycetee, folly, ignorance, simplicity.

o, one, the same.

of, come, come away! have done!

offertorie, offertory.

office, office, secular employment.

offring, offering, the act of going up to the altar to present alms.

omelies, homilies.

Omer, Homer.

ones, once.

on-lyve, alive.

ook, oak.

oon, one, the same; *after oon,* always of the same high quality; *al ones,* all one, of the same mind.

or, before.

oriental, Eastern.

other, (adj.) second.

other (conj.) either, or, other.

othes, oaths.

oule, owl.

ounces, small bunches, straggling pieces.

outrageous, excessive, immoderate, violent.

outrely, utterly, entirely.

out-rydere, a 'rider abroad'; a monk who rode about inspecting farms, etc.

out-twyne, utter, 'twist out.'

over, upper.

overeste, outer.

over-al, everywhere.

overspradde, pret. sing., spread over, covered; from 'oversprede.'

owher, anywhere.

pace, to pass, go, proceed; surpass.

panter, fowling net.

papingay, popinjay, parrot, woodpecker.

paraunter, perhaps.

par, by.

parfit, perfect.

parten, share, part; depart.

Parthes, the Parthians.

parisshens, parishioners.

party, part, portion.

parvys, church-porch; but see note to Prol., l. 310.

pas, pace, walking-pace.

passen, to surpass, exceed.

passing, excellent, surpassing.

pay, pleasure, satisfaction; *more to pay*, more satisfactorily.

payens, pagans.

peire, pair, set.

pens, pence; silver pennies.

pere, peer, equal.

pere-jonette, early pear.

perled, studded.

pers, (adj.) Persian blue; blue-grey cloth.
persone, person, parson.
pestilence, the plague.
peyne, (verb) to take pains, endeavour.
Phebus, Phœbus Apollo, god of the sun.
philosophye, learning, knowledge.
piled, p.p., deprived of hair, very thin, bald.
pilwe-beer, pillow-case.
pin, pin, brooch.
pinche, to find fault with.
pinched, p.p., pleated; from 'pinche.'
pitaunce, pittance, reward.
pitous, compassionate, merciful, plaintive.
plat, flat, downright, certain.
playing, see 'pleying.'
plee, plea.
plentevous, plentiful.
plesaunce, pleasure, delight.
pleyen, to jest, make sport.
pleying, amusement, sport.
pleyn, full, complete, honest.
pleyne, to complain, lament.
plyt, plight, condition; *in good plyt*, in a good position.
point, point, position; *in good point*, in good condition; cf. *embonpoint*.
pomely, dappled.
popet, doll, puppet.
popelote, doll, poppet, darling.
poraille, poor people.
port, port, carriage, behaviour.
post, post, pillar of a hall or room.
pothecarie, apothecary.
poudre, dust, powder, gunpowder.
poudre-marchaunt, a kind of spice.
poure, to pore, look closely.
poynaunt, hot with spices, tasty, piquant.
practisour, practitioner.
prenten, to imprint.

present, immediately.

press, throng, crowd; *prees* (*Truth*, l. 4) the crowd of courtiers.

preve, to prove.

prevy, privy, unobserved.

preysinges, praise, honour, glory.

pricasour, hard rider.

priken, to incite, urge.

priking, tracking the hare by its footprints.

privee, (adj.) secret.

privee, (subst.) privy.

prively, privately.

proces, process, proceeding, process of time, matter.

propre, (adj.) own, especial.

prow, profit, advantage.

pryme, prime, the canonical hour, beginning at 6 a.m.; then the period from 6 till 9.

prys, price, value, reputation.

pulled, plucked.

pultrye, poultry.

purchacen, to procure, acquire.

purchas, gain, acquisition, proceeds of begging or stealing.

puchasour, conveyancer; *purchasing*, conveyancing.

purfiled, trimmed at the edges.

purpos, purpose, design.

purtreye, to draw.

purveyaunce, providence, foresight, provision.

pyk, pike.

quake, to tremble, shiver.

quarter, quarter; a fourth part of the night.

quek, quack.

quelle, to kill.

queynt, p.p., quenched; from 'quenche.'

queynt, strange, curious, dainty.

quik, alive.

quyte, to requite, reward.

radde, pret. sing., advised; from 'rede.'

rage, to romp, toy wantonly; become violent.

rage, madness, passion.

rampeth, pres. sing., rages; *rampeth in my face*, flies in my face.

rape, haste.

rascaille, mob.

rather, former.

raughte, pret. sing., reached; from 'reche.'

ravyne, ravening, greediness; *foules of ravyne*, birds of prey.

real, royal, regal.

rebel, rebellious.

recche, to reck, care, heed.

recorde, to record, witness, bear in mind, bring to remembrance.

recreant, confessing himself defeated.

rede, (adj.) red.

rede, (subst.) counsel.

rede, (verb) to read, advise, counsel, interpret.

redily, quickly, promptly.

reed, (adj.) red.

reed, (subst.) counsel, advice.

refreyd, cooled down.

regne, kingdom, realm, dominion.

reherce, to rehearse, repeat.

rehersinges, repetitions.

rekening, reckoning, account.

rekke, first person, pres. sing., care.

relik, relic.

renne, to run.

renning, running; *at a renning*, at a run.

rente, revenue, income; *to rente*, as a tribute.

repeyre, to repair, return.

replicacioun, reply.

reportour, reporter, judge, referee.

repreve, reproof.

reprevable, reprehensible.

reson, reason, right, argument, opinion, order.

respect, to, in respect.

retracciouns, retractions, things withdrawn.

reve, to take away, rob.

revel, revelry.

reverence, of greet, greatly respected.

reward, regard, attention; *having reward to,* considering.

rewe, to have pity, be sorry.

rewthelees, pitiless, merciless.

reysed, p.p., gone on a military expedition.

riche, rich people.

rightwisnesse, righteousness.

roche, rock.

rody, ruddy.

rood, pret. sing., rode; from 'ryde.'

roos, pret. sing., rose; from 'ryse.'

roost, roast.

ropen, p.p., reaped.

rote, root.

rote, rote; *by rote,* by heart.

rote, a stringed instrument, an early form of the violin.

roten, rotten; *roten-herted,* rotten-hearted.

rouncy, a large, strong horse; perhaps a post-horse.

route, company, band.

route, to snore.

routhe, pity, compassion, mercy.

rowe, (adv.) roughly, angrily.

rowthe, ruth, pity.

royalliche, royally; with pomp.

rudeliche, rudely; *rudeliche and large,* roughly and freely.

ruled, well-mannered.

ryde, to ride; *ryden out,* to go on a military expedition.

ryot, riotous living.

ryve, to pierce, thrust.

sad, stable, firm, sober, serious.

sangwyn, blood-red; red cloth (Prol., l. 439)

sat, on knees she; she fell on her knees.

sautrye, psaltery, a kind of harp.

savour, impers. sing., taste, have relish for; from 'savoure.'

savorous, sweet, pleasant.

sawcefleem, covered with pimples.

scalle, scab.

scalled, p.p., scabby, scurfy.

scarsly, parsimoniously.

scathe, harm, misfortune.

science, knowledge, learning.

scole, school, manner, fashion.

scoleye, to study.

scriveyn, scrivener, scribe.

scrivenish, like a scrivener, professional letter-writer.

secree, (adj.) secret, trustworthy.

seke, sick, ill.

sely, innocent, simple, poor, wretched; but also happy, kind, good.

semely, becomingly.

semi-cope, short outer cape or cloak.

sendal, thin silk.

sentement, feeling, sentiment.

sentence, meaning, drift.

sepulture, grave, tomb.

sermone, to preach, speak.

servisable, willing to serve.

servyse, service, serving.

set, pret. sing., has sat, is sitting; from 'sitten.'

sethe, to seethe, boil.

seurtee, surety, security.

seyl, sail.

seyntes, saints.

shaltow, shalt thou.

shamfastnesse, modesty, shyness.

shap, shape, form.

shapen, to plan, devise.

shaply, fit.

shende, to disgrace, destroy.

shene, bright, fair.

shine, shin.

shirreve, sheriff.

sho, shoe.

shoon, pret. sing., shone; from 'shyne.'

shoop, planned; from 'shapen'; *so shoop it*, it so happened.

shorte, to shorten; *to shorte with your weye,* to shorten your way with.

shortly, briefly.

short-sholdred, with short upper arms.

shrewe, scoundrel, wretch.

shrewedness, wickedness.

shuldres, shoulders.

sikerly, surely, certainly.

sikernesse, security, safety.

silver, often used generically for 'money.'

simple, modest, innocent.

sin, since.

singe, to sing.

sinwes, sinews.

sit, it, it is fitting.

sith, (conj.) since; (adv.) afterwards, then.

sittingest, most fitting.

skile, reason, cause.

skilful, reasonable.

slee, sleen, to slay, kill.

sleep, pret. sing., slept; from 'slepe.'

sleighte, trickery.

sleeth, pres. sing., slays, kills; from 'slee.'

slombringe, slomeringe, slumber.

sloo, sloe.

slough, pret. sing., slew; from 'slee.'

slouthe, sloth.

sluggy, sluggish.

smal, small, delicate; fine in tone (of a voice).

smerte, (adv.) smartly, shapely.

smerte, (verb) to smart, feel pain.

smoot, pret. sing., smote; from 'smyte.'

snewed, pret. sing., snowed, abounded.

snibben, to chide, rebuke.

sober, grave, solemn; *soberly,* gravely, with a melancholy air.

sojorne, to dwell, stay.

solas, amusement, comfort, diversion.

solempne, formal, ceremonious, impressive.

soleyn, solitary, unmated.

somdel, somewhat.

sonded, sanded.

sondry, various.

sone, (adv.) soon.

sone, (subst.) son.

songe, p.p., sung; from 'singe.'

sonne, sun.

sooth, truth.

soothfastnesse, truth.

soothly, truly.

sop, sop (of bread), *sop in wyn*, wine with bread soaked in it.

sophistrye, evil, cunning.

sore, to soar.

sort, lot, chance, destiny.

sorted, pret. sing., allotted.

sorwe, sorrow, grief.

sote, sweet.

sothe, sooth, truth.

sothly, truly.

soule, by my fader, by my father's soul.

soun, sound.

soune, to sound, utter.

souninge, relating to, inclining to.

souple, supple, pliant.

sours, source, origin; swift upward flight.

sovereyn, supreme, chief.

sowne, sound.

spare, to spare, refrain.

sparwe, sparrow.

special, in, especially, particularly.

spede, to succeed.

speed, help, success.

spere, spear.

spere, sphere, orbit, globe.

sperhauk, sparrow-hawk.

sperred, p.p., barred.

spille, to spill, drop; destroy, ruin.

spoon, spone, spoon.

P

spores, spurs.

sporne, to spurn, kick.

sprad, p.p., spread, opened; from 'sprede.'

sprede, to spread, open.

spyced, p.p., spiced, scrupulous; sophisticated, pliable.

Stace, Statius.

stal, pret. sing., stole; from 'stelen.'

stant, pres. sing., stands; from 'stonde.'

starf, pret. sing., died; from 'sterve.'

stark, strong.

stat, state, condition.

stel, steel.

stelen, to steal; *stal,* pret. sing., stole.

stellifye, to make into a constellation.

stemed, pret. sing., shone, gleamed.

stenten, to stop, leave off.

stepe, bright, glittering.

stere, to steer, control; stir, move.

sterlinges, sterling coins.

sterre, star.

sterve, to die.

stevene, voice, sound.

stewe, fish-pond.

stewes, brothels.

steyre, staircase.

stiked, pret. sing., stuck; from 'stiken.'

stif, strong, bold.

stille, quiet, still.

stiwardes, stewards.

stoon, stone.

stoor, store, stock of a farm.

storven, pret. plural, died; from 'sterve.'

stot, stallion, horse, cob.

straunge, strange, foreign.

strawen, to strew.

streit, narrow.

streite, (adv.) tightly.

stremes, currents.

streng, string.
strike, hank (of flax).
stronde, strand, shore.
stryving, strife.
studie, to study, meditate, muse.
subgit, subject.
subtilly, craftily.
suffisaunce, sufficiency, contentment.
surquidrie, arrogance, presumption.
sustene, to sustain, support.
swalwe, swallow.
swappe, swoop (of a bird of prey).
swerd, sword.
sweven, dream.
swevening, dream.
swich, such.
swink, labour, toil.
swinke, to labour, toil.
swinker, worker.
swote, sweet.
swoune, to swoon, faint.
swow, swoon.
swythe, quickly.
syke, to sigh.
sythe, time; *ofte sythes*, many times.

tabard, herald's coat of arms; labourer's loose coat.
table, table; *table dormant*, permanent table.
taffata, taffeta, thin glossy silk.
taille, tally, an account scored on notched sticks.
takel, tackle, gear, weapons, especially arrows.
tale, to tell a tale, talk.
talent, inclination, wish.
tapicer, tapestry weaver.
tappestere, female tapster, barmaid.
targe, target, shield.
tart, pungent, sharply flavoured.
tempest thee, violently distress yourself.

Temple, Inn of Court.
temporeles, temporal.
tene, vexation, grief.
tercel, male eagle.
terme, set time, appointed time.
termes, technical terms.
termyne, to determine.
that, that which.
thee, to thrive, prosper; *so thee'ch,* as I hope to prosper.
ther, there, where, wherever.
ther-as, there where, where.
ther-to, besides, moreover.
ther-with-al, thereupon.
thider, thither.
thikke, thick, stout.
thilke, that.
thing, legal document (Prol. l. 325).
tho, (plural) those.
tho, (adv.) then.
thral, thrall, slave.
thridde, third.
thrift, success, welfare.
thriftily, carefully.
thrifty, profitable, careful.
thrye, thrice.
thryve, to thrive, prosper.
tikelnesse, instability.
til, to.
tipet, tippet, cape.
to, too.
to-cleve, to cleave in twain.
tollen, to take toll.
tombesteres, female tumblers, dancing-girls.
tonne, tun, barrel, cask.
to-rende, to tear in pieces.
torn, (subst.) turn.
tornen, to turn.
to-shivered, p.p., been broken to pieces.

to-tere, pret. plural, tear in pieces.

tough, make it, to make a display by using arguments

toun, town, village.

Tour, the Tower of London.

tragedie, tragedy, tragic story.

trays, traces.

trespasse, to trespass, transgress.

tretee, treaty.

tretys, well-proportioned, graceful.

treye, three.

trist, subst., trust.

triste, to trust.

trompe, trumpet.

trone, throne.

trouthe, truth, troth.

trowen, to believe.

tukked, tucked.

tunge, tongue.

turtel, turtle-dove.

turves, turf-plots.

tweye, two.

twinne, to sever, part, depart.

tyd, time, hour.

tydif, tidy, a small bird.

tyne, barrel, cask.

uncircumscript, unbounded, boundless.

unconninge, ignorance.

uncouth, strange, foreign.

undergrowe, of short stature.

undertake, to affirm; conduct an enterprise.

unkindely, unnaturally.

unlust, disinclination.

unnethes, scarcely.

upright, upright; lying on one's back.

utterly, entirely, fully.

vache, cow, beast.

vavasour, sub-vassal; substantial landowner.

venerye, hunting.

verdit, verdict.

vermin, mammals injurious to game and crops.

vernicle, vernicle; the reproduction of Christ's face on St Veronica's handkerchief.

verray, very, true.

verrayly, verily, truly.

verre, glass.

vertu, virtue, power; vital energy.

veyl, our lady, Our Lady's veil; the veil of the Virgin Mary.

veyne, vein.

viage, voyage, journey.

vicaire, vicar, deputy.

vigilyes, vigils, meetings on the eve of a festival.

vileinye, shameful conduct, unfit speech, rudeness, ill-breeding.

vitaille, victuals, provisions.

voluper, night-cap, woman's cap.

vouche, to call, declare; *vouche sauf*, to grant, permit.

voyden, to go away; remove, expel.

wafereres, makers of wafer-cakes, confectioners.

wake, to be awake, lie awake.

walken, to walk, roam.

walwed, p.p., immersed; from 'walwe.'

wan, pret. sing., won; from 'winne.'

wanhope, despair.

wantownesse, wantonness, mannerism of speech, affectation.

war, prudent, cautious, aware; *beth war*, be careful, beware.

waraunte, to warrant.

war him, let him beware.

waryce, to heal, cure.

wastel-breed, cake-bread, bread of the best quality.

waterlees, waterless.

wawe, wave.

waxen, to become.

wayten, to lie in wait for, watch, observe.

webbe, weaver.

weel, well.

weder, weather.

welawey, alas!

weldy, active.

wele, happiness, success, prosperity.

welked, withered.

wende, pret. sing., thought; from 'wenen.'

wenden, to go.

wenen, to suppose, imagine; *who wende*, pret. sing. subj., who would have thought. (Parsoner's Tale, l. 320).

went, p.p., gone; from 'wenden.'

wente, (subst.) turn, path.

werbul, tune.

werche, to work, perform.

werken, to work, act.

werre, war.

werreye, to make war.

wers, worse.

wesele, weasel.

weste; by weste, in the West of England.

weste, to turn to the west.

wether, sheep.

wex, wax.

wexen, to wax, grow, become.

wey, way; *do wey*, away with!

weyeden, pret. plural, weighed; from 'weyen.'

weymentinge, lamenting.

what, whatever, why.

whelkes, pimples, blotches.

whelp, puppy, cub.

wher, whether.

wher-as, where that, where.

whette, p.p., plural, sharpened.

whylom, once, formerly.

widwe, widow.

wight, person, creature, man.

wighte, weight.

wilful, wilfully.

wimpel, wimple, a covering for the head, pleated under the chin.
winde, to bend.
winke, to sleep.
winne, to win, gain, profit.
winsinge, skittish.
winter, years.
wissh, first person, pret. sing., washed; from 'wasshe.'
wiste, pret. sing., knew, expected; from 'witen.'
wit, reason, mind, intelligence.
witen, to know.
withouten, besides, as well as.
withholde, p.p., retained, maintained; from 'withholden.'
witing, knowledge.
wo, unhappy.
wode, wood, mad.
wol, first person, pret. sing., will.
wolle, wool.
wombe, belly.
wonder, (adj.) wonderful.
wonder, (adv.) wondrously.
wonderly, wondrously.
wone, (subst.) custom, usage.
wone, (verb) to dwell, inhabit.
woning, pres. part., dwelling; from 'wone.'
woning, habitation, house.
wood, mad.
woodnesse, madness.
woost, second pers. sing. knowest; from 'witen.'
woot, pres. sing., know; from 'witen.'
wot, pres. sing., knows; from 'witen.'
wrastling, wrestling.
wrawe, angry.
wrecche, (subst.) sorrowful creature, wretch.
wrecche, (adj.) wretched.
wreen, to cover, clothe.
wreke, to wreak, avenge.
wrighte, workman.
wroghte, pret. sing., acted; from 'werche.'

wroken, p.p., avenged; from 'wreke.'

wrooth, wroth, angry.

wrye, to hide, disguise, cover.

wyd, wide.

wyde, widely.

wyfhod, wifehood, womanhood.

wyn, wine.

wynt, pres. sing., turns, directs; from 'winde.'

wys, wise, prudent; *to make it wys*, to hold off, deliberate.

wyte, (subst.) to blame, reproach.

wyves, wives, women.

yaf, pret. sing., gave; from 'yeve.'

yate, gate.

y-be, p.p., been.

y-boren, p.p., born, carried; from 'bere.'

y-chaped, p.p., furnished with "chapes" or metal caps.

y-clept, p.p., called.

y-come, late, just come.

y-coyned, p.p., coined.

ydel, in, in vain.

y-do, p.p., done, finished.

y-drawe, p.p., drawn.

ye, eye.

yeddinges, songs.

yeldhalle, guild-hall.

yelwe, yellow.

yeman, yeoman; *yemanly*, in yeoman-like fashion.

yerde, rod, stick.

yeve, to give; *yeving*, giving.

y-falle, p.p., fallen.

y-fere, p.p., together.

y-go, p.p., gone.

y-grave, p.p., cut, graven.

y-hed, p.p., hidden.

y-hent, p.p. seized, caught.

y-hight, p.p., called.

yis, yes.

yit, yet.

yive, to give.

y-knowe, p.p., known.

y-lad, p.p., led, carried.

y-liche, y-like, alike, similar.

y-loren, p.p., lost.

y-nogh, enough; often used in the sense of 'much,' 'a great deal.'

y-nome, p.p. caught, overcome.

yond, yonder.

yore, ful, for a long time past.

y-preved, p.p., proved.

y-ronne, p.p., run.

y-shave, p.p., shaved.

y-shrive, p.p., shriven, absolved.

y-slawe, p.p., slain.

y-teyed, p.p., tied, pulled up.

y-wimpled, p.p., wearing a wimple.

y-wis, certainly, truly.

y-wounde, p.p., wound, covered up.

y-wroght, p.p., made.

y-wroken, p.p., avenged.